VOLUME I OF THE CONNOLLY TAROT

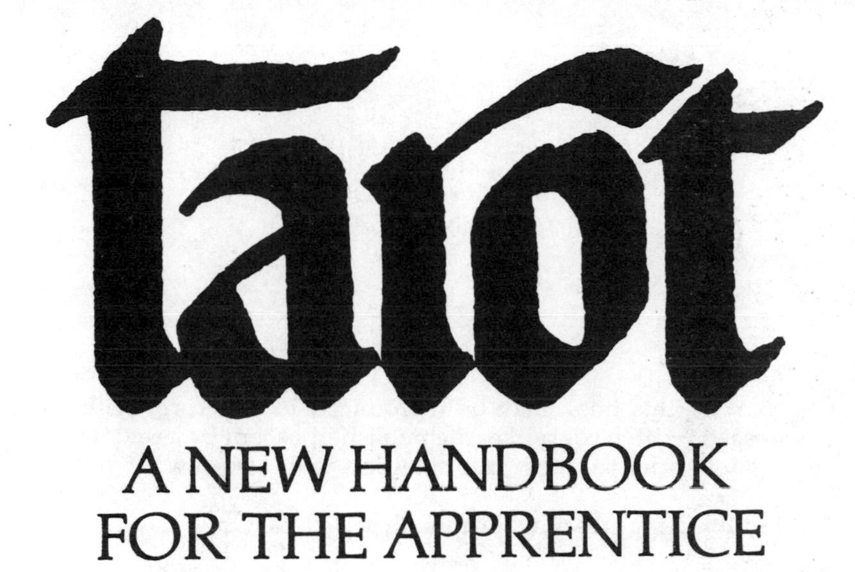

A NEW HANDBOOK FOR THE APPRENTICE

EILEEN CONNOLLY

Gnothi Seauton (Know Thyself).
— attributed to Thales
(c 624 - 546 B.C.)

NEWCASTLE PUBLISHING COMPANY INC.

NORTH HOLLYWOOD, CALIFORNIA
1979

ISBN 0-87877-045-3

Edited by Douglas Menville and Alyce Tulips.

Library of Congress Cataloging in Publication Data

Connolly, Eileen.
Tarot : a new handbook for the apprentice.

1. Tarot. I. Title.
BF1879.T2C58 133.3'2424 79-15303
ISBN 0-87877-345-2
ISBN 0-87877-045-3 pbk.

FIRST EDITION

A NEWCASTLE BOOK

First Printing October 1979

14

Printed in the United States of America

To Leena-Maija

EDITORS' NOTE

For this second printing (May 1980) several minor corrections have been made and omissions rectified.

PREFACE

The object of this Handbook is to offer not only a spiritual apprenticeship to students of the Sacred Tarot but to offer a concise reference for anyone interested in investigating and interpreting the fascinating symbology of the Tarot in relation to the Cabala, Astrology and the esoteric science of Numerology. The Handbook is divided into three sections:

Section 1 Basic lessons, exercises, procedures, meditations and fundamental esoteric philosophy relating to the Major and Minor Arcana.

Section 2 Major and Minor Mentors, which are guides to the positive and negative interpretations of the symbols on each card. Further Mentor guidelines include a Comparison Chart and an in-depth explanation of meanings when certain symbols fall near each other in a spread.

Section 3 Procedures necessary prior to spreading the cards for divination.

My intention is to teach you as simply as possible how to work with and understand the Tarot cards, and not to attempt at this stage to fill your mind with too much unnecessary detail. I would like you to feel that I am teaching you personally, so that the Handbook becomes not only a source of learning but a friend you can relate to on a very personal level. During my years of teaching the esoteric sciences, I have found that people usually want to "get on with it" as soon as possible, so I intend to present the rudiments of this ancient art to you right away. It is important for the beginner to become involved with the symbology of the Tarot deck immediately; once you are familiar with the cards and feel able to master the basic procedures, your enthusiasm will be aroused and you will be motivated to learn all you can. It is at this point that the real adventure of Tarot begins.

Whatever your purpose in studying the Tarot may be, this Handbook will provide you with a continual ready reference. It contains both method and procedure for learning the art of divination. By using the Major and Minor Mentor guides, you will be able to locate Cabalistic, Astrological and Numerological references at a glance. Each individual subject is treated in such a way as to enable you to quickly discover and explore whatever aspect of the Tarot you desire.

Eileen Connolly

Santa Barbara, California
December, 1978

CONTENTS

Preface		v
List of Charts		viii
List of Exercises		ix
Author's Note		x
Introduction		1
A Note on Procedure		3
SECTION I		
Chapter 1	Beginning Your Apprenticeship	7
Chapter 2	Learning the Minor Arcana	17
Chapter 3	Learning the Court Cards	29
Chapter 4	Learning the Major Arcana	39
SECTION II		
Chapter 5	Understanding the Minor Mentors	61
Chapter 6	Understanding the Minor Mentors	71
Chapter 7	The Minor Mentors	77
Chapter 8	The Court Mentors	145
Chapter 9	The Major Mentors	163
SECTION III		
Chapter 10	Steps to Divination	211
Chapter 11	How to Read the Cards	219
Chapter 12	The Esoteric Time Cards	233
Chapter 13	Beginning and End	243
	Index of Cards	244

LIST OF CHARTS

Chart 1	Daily Record Book	13
Chart 2	Minor Sequence Table	19
Chart 3	Thought Track	25
Chart 4	Tarot Log	56
Chart 5	Cabalastic Reference —Major Arcana	73
Chart 6	The Tree of Life	74
Chart 7	Lemniscate for Divination	220
Chart 8	Celtic Cross Spread	223
Chart 9	Celtic Block Spread	228
Chart 10	Predictive Manteia Spread	230
Chart 11	Time Chart	236

LIST OF EXERCISES

Exercise	1	Esoteric Approach to Suit Keys	21
Exercise	2	Random Selection of Suit Keys	22
Exercise	3	Esoteric Approach to the Aces	23
Exercise	4	Thought Track	26
Exercise	5	Synthesizing the Seed with the Suit Key	26
Exercise	6	Sensitivity Key to Court Cards	30
Exercise	7	Court Cards on the Thought Track	36
Exercise	8	Daily Prayer with the Major Arcana	40
Exercise	9	The Spiritual Path of the Major Arcana	50
Exercise	10	Entering the Major Arcana	57
Exercise	11	Analysis of the Celtic Cross	223

AUTHOR'S NOTE

Many of my previous students will immediately realize that here is a higher esoteric interpretation for each Tarot symbol, as promised. I sincerely hope that their spiritual vision may be enhanced and that these lessons will give even greater satisfaction than the preliminary lessons of the past.

INTRODUCTION
GNOTHI SEAUTON = KNOW THYSELF

It has been said that the Tarot cards contain the secrets of the universe. It is only through the discovery of your own hidden depths that you may explore the Higher Spiritual Self and begin to learn these secrets. When you allow sensitivity of the soul to open the door, the ancient symbols of the Tarot will reveal their mysteries to you.

The best way to commence your studies is to work to discard inner conflicts and impatience. A new student can easily become confused and discouraged trying to absorb the varied interpretations and sometimes conflicting theorics of the Tarot's origin and history. The reason for these apparent contradictions is that each Tarot Master has expressed personal conclusions, based on his own experience and study, independent of other opinions. It is advisable, therefore, to approach the Tarot with an open mind. Once you have experienced the fascinating accuracy of divination and have learned how to read the ancient symbols with sensitivity, you will be ready for in-depth study. Until then, be content to learn at your own pace and enjoy the awakening of your own psychic abilities as you take your journey as an apprentice down the Royal Road of Tarot.

Behind the intriguing disguise of the Tarot deck is the entrance to an astonishing dimension of occult wisdom. Throughout the ages, simple uncluttered souls have been able to enjoy the benefits of hidden wisdom naturally and easily, perhaps because they could readily accept God's laws and had respect for the eternal soul of man. Children can often let go and wander at will in the higher realms. Perhaps many of us today are too bogged down with a "prove it" kind of attitude, thus making us totally unprepared to receive the guidance of our Higher Self. Intuition, an absolutely natural sense, is slowly becoming extinct from lack of use. Until we learn again to trust our own inner feelings, we will be forced to live in the limitations of practical thought, which does not allow us to expand our consciousness beyond everyday affairs.

Whenever we attempt to approach our Higher Self by using our powers of reason and intellect, we always arrive at a point of utter confusion and frustration. We can go to great lengths to find reasons for this dilemma, we can philosophize with each other, but we always arrive at the same conclusion eventually. The dilemma will be solved once we realize that the key to self knowledge is pure simplicity. We must relax not only the body, but the busy mind, letting go of everyday problems and concerns, allowing the higher vibrations to flow through our mind and body.

Unfortunately, when we do have an opportunity to unwind and make contact with our Higher Self, we often try to wrestle with our problems on a conscious level, striving to manipulate and solve them completely on our own. With the right attitude, we can rise to the Higher Consciousness and achieve a level of peace, balance and harmony, wherein the solutions to our problems will come to us naturally and our anxieties will be overcome.

With practice, you can achieve this state of mind at will, like other students before you. But you may feel that you have tried this before, that it doesn't work for you. If so, you probably haven't tried long enough or hard enough, or under the right conditions. Choose a time when you are not too tired, for instance. When you are physically or mentally exhausted, you are apt to allow your mind to drift backwards and forwards over the day's activities and eventually fall asleep amidst this inner whirlpool. This results in your waking up so tired that you feel you haven't been to sleep at all.

When you are not tired, you can achieve the physical and mental relaxation which is a prerequisite to probing the higher realms of consciousness, and can exert direction and will toward this endeavor. Approach it as you would any other activity intended to give you pleasure. Be alert and ready to tackle whatever lies ahead. Be objective and use the exercises in this Handbook as you would any educational instruction. This attitude will help you speed your goal of inner realization, a goal which should be that of all men: *Gnothi seauton*—Know thyself.

A NOTE ON PROCEDURE

What Do You Do with Tarot Cards?

This question is simple and direct, but I'm afraid the answer is more complex. To avoid getting into areas of philosophy not relevant to our early studies, I will attempt an answer within the context of this Handbook. Tarot cards can be used for:

1. Divination, either for self reading or for another person*
2. Self guidance
3. Meditation
4. Spiritual development
5. Cabalistic studies.

The apprentice should read the entire Handbook through once; then start at the beginning and pursue all the exercises at his or her own pace. For the more experienced student, there are interesting exercises and theories relating the Tarot to the Cabala, Astrology and Gnothology, or esoteric Numerology.

It is my sincere hope that the reader will spend many happy and constructive hours with this Handbook. It has been prepared so that it may be continually used throughout the course of study for reference and practice.

* Divination may be defined as obtaining knowledge of the unknown or of the future.

SECTION I

CHAPTER 1
BEGINNING YOUR APPRENTICESHIP

It is not my intention to delve at great length into the history of the Tarot, nor offer my own theories regarding its origin. This has been done by other authors and teachers, who have produced many excellent works for the student interested in these areas. My purpose in writing this Handbook is to help you understand the ancient symbology of the Tarot and to appreciate the esoteric beauty and wisdom of this ancient art.

We will begin with the pictures portrayed on the cards. In your search for the proper deck of Tarot cards, you will notice that there are many variations in design. All of them represent the same thing—the esoteric symbology that has come down to us from antiquity. It is not the picture itself that should interest you so much as the symbolic philosophy behind the picture and how the picture affects you personally.

Each of the Tarot decks has come from different avenues of thought embracing other metaphysical sciences. Each has been influenced by the source and principles of the particular knowledge from which it is derived. Yet all of their roots coalesce to offer personal guidance and direction from the higher levels of consciousness. Each of the artists has portrayed his or her own interpretation of the spiritual force.

The form and nature of the Tarot symbols are still secrets known fully only to highly developed souls. As an initiate of the higher orders, you must be strict with yourself in moral, ethical and spiritual codes. You shoud study and understand the sciences of the Cabala, Astrology and Numerology. When you reach the dawn of understanding, you will be able to use your own personal tools to create your own spiritual masterpiece. Until that time arrives, be patient and learn the fundamentals that will enable you to develop the skills of a Tarot Master. Once you are conversant with the Tarot and its symbols and are able to relate its occult wisdom to your own life, you may find that the history of the Tarot is of more interest to you.

Ancient Beginnings

Hermetic tradition believes the earliest records of Tarot to be about 35,000 years old. It has been said that the Tarot decks which evolved in successive centuries were not completely true representations of the Universal Law. This is very likely, considering how the early Christian fathers established their dogma, hiding the esoteric knowledge to make way for man-made teachings which helped make life more comfortable for those in power. Unfortunately, ordinary men had not evolved far enough spiritually to fully understand the laws emanating from the *Ain Soph* (Supreme Being) without interpretation by teachers. So the Sacred Truths, forbidden to the many, were preserved by the few, handed down through the centuries in secret societies and brotherhoods, under the direction of initiated Keepers of the Flame. The Ancient Wisdom has thus been propagated through these limited channels to those who undergo vigorous mental, physical and spiritual training before the Truths are revealed to them. Each member must serve an apprenticeship, during which he or she learns discipline in all things, including the absolute riddance of the false ego. The apprentice lives a life of truth and purity, obeying the Higher Spiritual Consciousness, rather than being influenced by the dictates and expectations of other men. With this discipline comes the loneliness of often not being understood by others, even loved ones, but this is balanced by the joy of knowing that it does not matter when one is understood by God.

Perhaps the time is not far off when the entire body of Ancient Wisdom will be revealed at last to all men. Hermetic tradition tells of two major secrets yet to be discovered beneath the Great Pyramid of Gizeh. It is said that a hidden temple contains magnificent tablets on which are inscribed the totality of the Universal Law concerning the soul's journey through the cycle of rebirth. Seventy-eight of these tablets are known as the "exoteric" Tarot and 30 are the "esoteric" Tarot—a total of 108 tablets revealing at last the mystery and purpose of the soul.

Now, from our brief look at the past and future, let's come back to the present, where you are ready to take the first step on your own journey down the Royal Road of Tarot.

Handling Your Tarot Cards

Buying your first pack of Tarot cards is like buying a packet of seeds. You cannot expect flowers to grow overnight; you must plant and nourish the seeds and wait patiently for the blooms to appear. Adopt this same attitude with your Tarot cards and you will be pleasantly surprised at how quickly your esoteric seeds will bloom. Remember that the more you study and the more you handle the cards, the quicker you will begin to make spiritual progress.

There are probably several book stores in your area that stock a variety of Tarot decks; most larger cities now have at least one book store that specializes in spiritual and occult books. A look through your local Yellow Pages should reveal its location. If not, you may order your deck through the mail: I would suggest that you write to U.S. Games Systems, Inc., 468 Park Avenue South, New York, NY 10016. They stock the largest and most complete line of Tarot decks and books in the country, and at your request, will send you a lovely color catalog of these items.

Although you may choose any of the various decks that appeal to you, I recommend the use of the "Rider Waite Tarot Deck," named after the world-famous occult scholar and author, Dr. Arthur Edward Waite, who produced the deck in 1910. The designs were drawn and colored under his supervision by Pamela Coleman Smith, an American girl who was a fellow member of the occult society, the Order of the Golden Dawn.

Through teaching many classes and seminars in Tarot, I have found the Waite Deck to be the most suitable for beginners. Its beauty and simplicity stimulate students and allow them to learn at a faster pace. This is the deck you will see illustrated later on in this Handbook.

After purchasing your deck, handle the cards as often as you can. When they are new they feel much different from a deck that has been "seasoned," that is, fully saturated with your own personal vibrations. For example, a Tarot Master usually has a minimum of two seasoned packs and would never attempt to perform a divination with a new deck.

Furthermore, once you begin to season your own deck, you must never allow another person to handle it, as this will disturb your own vibratory bond to the deck by mixing up his or her vibrations with yours.

I once knew a student who, upon arriving home from a journey of over a hundred miles, immediately turned her car around when she discovered she had forgotten her Tarot cards. Having used the cards during her stay at a friend's house, she knew that her hosts had been intrigued with the deck and would no doubt look through them. Rather than risk the vibratory disturbance this would cause, the student made the long return journey and thankfully arrived back at her hosts' home before they realized the cards had been left behind.

I always advise my students to carry their packs with them in a pocket or purse, wrapped in a protective silk cloth. I also recommend that you sleep with them under your pillow, which further aids in their impregnation with your vibrations. When you are home watching television, take the opportunity to handle the cards, move them around, shuffle them any way you wish. You need not concentrate on what you're doing—your Higher Self will be subconsciously preparing the cards for your work with the Tarot. Don't be concerned if you notice the cards falling in reverse positions—let them fall naturally into any position. This is necessary in order to season the deck correctly. Never go through the pack putting any particular card in any particular order or changing it to an upright position.

Handling the cards must continue until you become aware that your vibrations have thoroughly permeated the deck. How long this will take depends on how often you handle the cards and how serious you are about learning the Tarot. The more you manipulate the deck, the sooner you will begin to receive your first esoteric impressions, which will be a signal that you are ready to proceed.

Preparing for Divination

Nothing is more frustrating than to be ready to start a spread (laying out the cards for divination) and to find that you haven't prepared everything you need. Check the list of requirements below—it includes everything you need initially to begin work with the cards. For best results, make sure that you have all these items on hand before you proceed:

1. Your Tarot deck
2. Silk scarf
3. Wooden box
4. Tarot cover
5. Wooden table
6. Daily Record Book

Your Tarot Deck

We've covered the selecting and preparing of your cards in the previous section. If you already own a pack of Tarot cards but have not used them correctly, or have left them lying around unprotected, I strongly suggest that you invest in a new deck and season them as I have mentioned earlier.

Silk Scarf

The natural fibres of a silk scarf or cloth protect your cards from outside vibrations when they are not in use. As soon as you purchase a new deck, you should discard the box they come in and transfer the cards to the protection of a silk cloth. Keeping them wrapped this way enhances the vibratory tone of your cards and makes them more conducive to accurate divination. Sound is tone, tone is color, color is vibration. Therefore, the color of the silk is very important. Gold, purple, or royal blue are excellent colors for attracting and retaining the level of energy around your Tarot deck. If you know your Soul Color, this is an obvious choice for the scarf. If possible, have the cloth ready to use before opening your new deck. Since the piece needed is not large, you can often buy beautiful remnants quite inexpensively from a fabric shop and finish them off nicely with pinking shears.

Wooden Box

After the cards are wrapped in the silk, they should be placed in a wooden box. The vibrations from natural wood are ideal for your Tarot deck, further protecting it from negative influences, so choose a box that appeals to you. Is it attractive to look at? Does it feel good to the touch? These things are important—your box will contain something very special in your life, so choose it well and be sure you are completely satisfied with your choice. Years ago, wooden boxes were hard to obtain, but nowadays they may be purchased inexpensively in large department stores and small gift shops.

Tarot Cover

The Tarot cover is another piece of cloth, also preferably silk, upon which to lay out your cards. It should be large enough to cover your Tarot table, or at least two feet square. Whenever you spread the cards, either for divination or study, always use the cover. If you are going to use the cards away from home, take your cloth cover with you—it may be used without the Tarot table. This will prevent you from picking up distracting influences in unfamiliar surroundings, a factor that will become more important to you as your sensitivity increases. As with the silk scarf, the Tarot cover should be either your Soul Color, gold, purple or royal blue.

Wooden Table

A wooden table is most desirable for laying out the cards, although wood is not absolutely essential unless the table is to be used *only* for the Tarot. I suggest that you *do* use a wooden table, and use it only for your card study and divination. The natural vibrations of the wood will increase your awareness and help you tune in to the higher energies. The table should be large enough to accommodate the different types of spreads we will discuss later—at least two feet square. When not in use, keep the table in your bedroom or in any fairly secluded corner of the house. Keep it covered with the Tarot cover, with a meditation candle and the wooden box containing your cards on top. Fresh flowers also add considerably to the vibratory tone; I like to have them near when working with the Tarot. Some of my students have made a Tarot table simply by purchasing a wooden top and attaching screw-on-type legs. If you have a choice of woods, choose pine, as this wood has been traditionally preferred by Tarot Masters down through the centuries.

Daily Record Book

While conducting a divination for yourself, you may receive information that you do not immediately understand. For this reason, I suggest that you keep a Daily Record Book to record systematically what you receive. I am often amazed to check back in my book and realize that true and accurate guidance has been given to me, although I didn't understand or appreciate it at the time. You may copy the example given as Chart 1 or type one of your own, following the example, and duplicate it as often as necessary. Keep the sheets in a loose-leaf notebook for easy reference. (We will discuss the different types of spreads and the use of the Major/Minor Pack later on, so don't be puzzled by these entries on the form.) This Daily Record Book is for those students who wish to record personal spreads only.

Remember that the Tarot should not be consulted too often—not more than once every 24 hours. A daily divination cannot be expected to have the same depth or significance as a weekly or monthly spread, but if you choose to work on a daily basis, create a rhythm with your readings. Conduct them at the same time every day and do the same with your meditation studies. Likewise, if you read weekly or monthly, do so at the same time each week or month.

DAILY RECORD BOOK

DATE: ____________________ **TIME:** ____________________

TYPE OF SPREAD: __________ **QUESTION:** __________

MAJOR/MINOR PACK: ______ ____________________

____

List cards in order of spread.

1 ____________________

2 ____________________

3 ____________________

4 ____________________

5 ____________________

6 ____________________

7 ____________________

8 ____________________

9 ____________________

10 ____________________

SKETCH SPREAD OR NOTES:

INTERPRETATION OF SPREAD:

CHART 1

Tools for Divination

One of the greatest temptations you will face is wanting to attempt divination, either for yourself or others, before you are really ready to do so. You must become familiar not only with the Tarot cards themselves, but with the skills needed to connect the symbols together and interpret what appears. The ability to extract and relate the full wisdom of the Tarot can only be achieved through study, concentration and development of sensitivity.

Just as a carpenter must learn to use his tools before he can make a cabinet or table, so you must become familiar with *your* tools—the 78 cards in the pack, plus the 78 Reverse Keys. This knowledge will enable you to interpret any message from the 156 Basic Keys, which in turn will provide access to the information in what we might call the Esoteric Computer. Individual Key interpretations must be pieced together before you can understand the whole picture, just as words are put together to form a sentence.

Mastering the symbols of the Major and Minor Arcana is the first step toward learning the Tarot. Learning the definitions for each card in both positive and reverse positions is important, but don't be discouraged if the desired sensitivity doesn't come at once. IT IS NOT WHAT YOU LEARN INITIALLY, BUT WHAT YOU ARE ABLE TO TUNE INTO EVENTUALLY that is most important in becoming a Tarot Master. Once your conscious mind stops struggling each time a different card is put down, you will be able to reach a level of relaxation which will allow the superconscious vibrations to flow smoothly into your conscious mind.

In order to comprehend the meaning of each symbol, both positive and negative, you must use the SUIT KEYS, which will be explained in the next chapter. Once you can bring to mind immediately the Key for each Tarot symbol, your conscious mind will relax and you will be in command of the esoteric alphabet. The cosmic energies will flow freely and you will be blessed with solutions to your problems drawn from your Higher Self.

Each of the 78 cards has a different meaning when it is reversed. This does *not* mean that a reversed card is negative in connotation or in opposition to the client's welfare. It simply means that there is a *different* interpretation to a card when it is reversed than when it falls right side up. I have had beginning students who thought that all they had to learn were interpretations for the 78 cards in upright positions, so that when they fell upside down, the interpretations were exactly the opposite. This is not correct. You are dealing in essence with 156 separate symbols, each with a distinct purpose which relates esoterically with both the card preceding it and the one following. A reverse card has an identity of its own and must be learned in the same manner as the upright or positive card.

The early masters of the Tarot did not have the modern addition of the 56 Minor Arcana; only the 22 Major Arcana were used for divination. The Major Arcana deal only with the spiritual aspect and eternal soul of man. But as man became more and more involved in his mundane existence, the Minor Arcana were added to the Tarot pack to help deal with matters pertaining to the physical plane. Thus, the Minor Arcana have become a useful addition for modern man in his everyday situations.

In the next chapter we will begin our study of the Minor Arcana and their meanings. At this point, let me emphasize that it is very important for you to follow the progression of this Handbook and not skip over the exercises that follow. Do them all in order and you will receive the greatest benefits. You may read through the entire Handbook at this point, if you wish, which will give you an overview that may prove helpful. Then come back to Chapter 2 and proceed toward EXERCISE 1.

If you are not the type of person who likes to do things alone, you may find it stimulating to form a group and study together. Each week, have a different person read the lesson aloud. Later, the group can pair off to practice divination. However you choose to proceed, keep in mind at all times the serious nature of your study. The Tarot is not a frivolous toy to show off with; it is a way of life and a means of gaining spiritual wisdom for the benefit of your own soul and for the well-being of others.

CHAPTER 2
LEARNING THE MINOR ARCANA

The Tarot deck is really two decks combined. These two decks are called the MAJOR ARCANA and the MINOR ARCANA.

22 cards = Major, or Greater Arcana
56 cards = Minor, or Lesser Arcana
78 cards = Total Tarot deck

You will notice that in the Rider Waite Deck, the Major Arcana are numbered I through XXI with roman numerals. The Fool, whose card is unnumbered (0), makes up the 22nd card. Now separate the cards of the Major Arcana from the rest of your deck and lay them aside. We will study them in Chapter 4.

The Minor Arcana are divided into four suits, just like a regular deck of playing cards, only instead of spades, clubs, hearts and diamonds, the four suits of the Tarot decks are:

WANDS
CUPS
SWORDS
PENTACLES

Note that Pentacles are sometimes referred to as COINS, because the pentacle is usually shown inside a round, coin-like shape. But the importance of this suit lies not in the coin, but in the pentacle, which is a potent occult symbol, very beneficent in the upright position. Note also that there is a distant correspondence between the Tarot suits and those of a modern deck of playing cards, evidence that the latter has descended in an abbreviated and bastardized form from the original Tarot deck.

WANDS = CLUBS
CUPS = HEARTS
SWORDS = SPADES
PENTACLES = DIAMONDS

As you study the Minor Arcana, you will notice further similarities between a modern deck and the Tarot pack. As for the Major Arcana, the Fool survives as the Joker, still considered outside the deck or a wild card.

Each of the four suits of the Tarot deck has a total of 14 cards:

ACE (1) 2 3 4 5 6 7 8 9 10 PAGE KNIGHT QUEEN KING = 14

Over the years, the Page and the Knight have been combined into one modern card, the Jack.

The Page, Knight, King and Queen are called COURT CARDS: later we will study them in more detail. Now, extract the Court Cards from the deck and lay them aside.

WANDS	PAGE KNIGHT QUEEN KING = 4
CUPS	PAGE KNIGHT QUEEN KING = 4
SWORDS	PAGE KNIGHT QUEEN KING = 4
PENTACLES	PAGE KNIGHT QUEEN KING = 4
	16 COURT CARDS

Now divide the remaining (40) Minor Arcana into the four suits of Wands, Cups, Swords and Pentacles. You will notice that in the Rider Waite Deck, each suit is numbered from II to X in roman numerals, with the Ace (1) unnumbered. (The Court Cards are also unnumbered.)

Next, examine the MINOR SEQUENCE TABLE on page 19. It will help to fix in your mind what each unit represents as a whole. This is extremely important—its importance will become more apparent as you begin to use the cards for divination.

MINOR SEQUENCE TABLE

	Tarot Suits.	English American Usage.	French.	French interpretation.	Italian	Italian interpretation.	German Symbols.	Seasons	Months.	Fixed Signs.	Elements.	Cardinal Points.
1	Wands.	Clubs.	Trefles	Trefoils.	Bastoni.	Batons.	Acorns	Summer.	June. July. August.	Taurus.	Fire.	South.
2	Cups.	Hearts.	Coeurs	Hearts.	Coppes.	Cups.	Hearts	Spring.	March. April. May.	Leo.	Water.	West.
3	Swords	Spades.	Piques.	Pikes.	Spade.	Sword.	Leaves.	Autumn.	Sept. October. November	Scorpio.	Air.	North.
4	Pentacles.	Diamonds	Carreaux	Paving Tiles.	Denari.	Coins.	Bells.	Winter.	Dec. Jan. Feb.	Aquarius.	Earth.	East.

	Sacred Name.	Sacred Word.	Esoteric Force.	Mythology	Ancient Celtic.	Alchemy	Function	Episcopal.	Suit Keys.	Activity	Principle.	Human Classes
1	I	Yod.	Male Active force.	Salamander	Spirit.	Mercury.	Intuition	Crosier.	Enterprise, Distinction	Fertility.	Substantiality.	Intellectual
2.	H	He.	Female Passive force.	Undine.	Soul.	Water.	Feeling.	Chalice.	Love, Happiness.	Emotion.	Imponderability	Professional
3.	V	Vau.	Union of Above forces.	Sylph.	Ego.	Sulphur.	Thinking.	Cross	Struggle, Animosity	Conquest	Triality.	Warrior.
4	H	He.	Physical Manifestation of Transition	Gnome.	Body.	Salt.	Sensation,	Host.	Money Interests.	Material Prosperity.	Perpetuation.	People.

CHART 2

For example, you can see from studying this chart that

A profusion of WANDS in a divination spread would generally indicate a situation involving ENTERPRISE AND DISTINCTION.

A profusion of CUPS would indicate LOVE AND HAPPINESS.

A profusion of SWORDS would indicate STRUGGLE AND ANIMOSITY.

A profusion of PENTACLES would indicate MONEY INTERESTS.

Not only do the individual cards combine to reveal information, but you will observe a general overall aspect from the predominance of any one suit in a spread.

To help you keep these associations in mind, you should commit to memory the following SUIT KEYS, which are the associations the cards possess on the material level:

WANDS = ENTERPRISE & DISTINCTION
CUPS = LOVE & HAPPINESS
SWORDS = STRUGGLE & ANIMOSITY
PENTACLES = MONEY INTERESTS

Take each individual suit in turn and concentrate only on the appropriate SUIT KEY. Try to sense the vibration surrounding the cards; meditate on the associations daily, until you reach the point at which the association automatically enters your mind whenever you see or think about the appropriate suit. Once you have achieved this, you are ready to try the esoteric approach in EXERCISE 1 on page 20.

Pick up one suit of ten cards and while holding them, close your eyes and concentrate for a few moments on its SUIT KEY. Try to take upon yourself the characteristics of the SUIT KEY—imagine yourself experiencing feelings of enterprise and distinction, love and happiness, struggle and animosity, or whatever is appropriate for the cards you have chosen. Take your time and try to build the SUIT KEY around you, like an actor assuming a role.

When you have accomplished this with one suit, repeat the experience with each of the other suits. Then lay all four suits before you on a table and pick them up at random, each time firmly implanting the vibratory influence of their SUIT KEYS in your mind. Holding and handling the cards while you concentrate will greatly help to build this sensitivity.

After you have done this repeatedly for a few days, you should be able to select any of the four suits at random and feel the appropriate SUIT KEY response. Having the ability to feel the four SUIT KEYS will provide a substantial foundation for further study, much as learning how to draw provides a foundation for an illustrator or a realist painter.

If you work with a partner, have him or her give you the names of the different suits, and as you hear them, pick up the cards and name the SUIT KEYS. Don't rush—allow enough time to really *feel* the vibrations of the SUIT KEYS, for you are combining *sensitivity* with *memory*, rather than merely memorizing by rote. This exercise, done properly, conscientiously and consistently, will develop your intuitive ability to a great degree.

When you feel you have achieved the proper associations, you are ready to perform the exercises which appear on the following pages.

EXERCISE 1: ESOTERIC APPROACH TO SUIT KEYS

1. Make sure your surroundings are comfortable, quiet and restful. Relax as completely as you can.
2. Select the suit of your choice.
3. Select a card at random from the suit.
4. Holding it before you, slowly and firmly repeat to yourself the appropriate SUIT KEY.
5. Continue to repeat the SUIT KEY as you slowly bring the card up to your Inner Eye, the spiritual center located between the eyebrows at the top of the nose.
6. Hold the card against your Inner Eye for a few seconds, implanting the SUIT KEY vibrations firmly in this area.
7. Then lower the card to your Solar Plexus, the front center of the body, located just below the rib cage.
8. Allow the feeling of the SUIT KEY to flow through you.

As you did this exercise, you should have experienced the feelings of the suit the card belonged to. For example, if you chose the THREE OF CUPS, you should have felt warm, loving vibrations flowing through you as you tuned in to the SUIT KEY for Cups, LOVE & HAPPINESS.

This esoteric approach to study practice is the best way to stimulate your Higher Mind and allow your intuition to blossom in your pursuit of the Tarot's wisdom. When you can comfortably go through EXERCISE 1 using any card from the Minor Arcana (except the Court Cards) at random, tuning in smoothly to any of the SUIT KEYS, you are ready to go on to EXERCISE 2.

EXERCISE 2: RANDOM SELECTION OF SUIT KEYS

1. Same as Step 1 in Exercise 1.
2. Shuffle the 40 cards well.
3. Lay the pack face down on the table or Tarot cloth.
4. Turn the cards over one at a time, tuning in to the appropriate SUIT KEY for each card.

EXERCISES 1 and 2 should not be hurried. Since it will take some time to go through all 40 cards, try to pick a time when you will not be disturbed. Early in the morning is especially good. Practice EXERCISE 2 each day, until you have mastered the ability to tune in to the SUIT KEYS for all 40 cards at random.Now you are well on your way to complete mastery of the Tarot.

Aces

The Ace is the first card of each suit; it generally represents
THE BEGINNING = THE SEED

However, this beginning or seed is *not always readily apparent* in a spread. This beginning or seed can be

SEEN OR UNSEEN = KNOWN OR UNKNOWN = GOOD OR BAD
Place the four Aces before you and imagine that they are the strings of a musical instrument. Gently run your fingers across the Aces and sense the vibrations of each of the four SUIT KEYS. Feel the changing moods as you tune in to each SUIT KEY, the heights and depths, the love and struggle. Experience the change of energies and emotions as your fingertips tune into this esoteric "melody." The Aces are very important to any spread, and you must learn to become especially sensitive to them and the seeds of events they contain.

On the next page you will find EXERCISE 3, an esoteric approach to the Aces.

EXERCISE 3: ESOTERIC APPROACH TO THE ACES

1. Same as Step 1 in EXERCISE 1.
2. Pick up the Ace of Wands and bring it up to your Inner Eye.
3. Feel the mysterious seed of THE BEGINNING OF ENTERPRISE AND DISTINCTION coming to life and growing.
4. Holding the card to your Inner Eye firmly, say: "BEGINNING OF ENTERPRISE AND DISTINCTION." Continue to concentrate and repeat these words until you feel that your conscious mind has accepted this esoteric Key. Let it penetrate deeply into your mind, feel that it is a part of you.
5. Still holding this thought and no other, lower the card to your Solar Plexus and begin to feel the Ace of Wands maturing within you. Let the energies of ENTERPRISE AND DISTINCTION flow through your body while you continue to repeat the SUIT KEY.
6. When both mind and body have merged in thought and sensitivity and you feel totally aware of this experience—then relax.
7. After a few moments, repeat Steps 2-5 with the remaining three Aces, each time tuning in to the proper SUIT KEY and being aware of the inner flow of energy as it develops and progresses through to your Higher Consciousness.

Preparation for the Thought Track

Learning requires complete concentration. Whenever we attempt to absorb information without concentrating fully, our conscious mind cannot retain it or recall it later when we need it. Everything we experience is constantly being filed in our subconscious, but it is not easily retrieved, and thus cannot always be utilized for our benefit whenever we wish.

Many intelligent people are so busy with insignificant day-to-day activities that they are never able to reach their fullest potential. Often they become frustrated and bitter, blaming other people or "circumstances" for their own lack of personal achievement or progress. We can avoid this pitfall by learning to concentrate fully on whatever project is at hand and allowing our subconscious mind to release the information we need when we need it. We must learn to discard those things in our lives that are time-consuming and unnecessary and focus our attention on those things which are essential to our physical, mental and spiritual well-being.

To help you achieve this concentration with regard to the Minor Arcana, I have constructed a THOUGHT TRACK (page 25) which provides a SEED PATTERN for the four Aces and the remainder of the Minor Arcana, including the Court Cards, as well. It will help you select a particular SEED for each card in the Minor Arcana, a SEED that has a special meaning to your Higher Self. Each card has its own SEED PATTERN, which is the esoteric pattern of the most important concepts symbolized by that card.

Let's take an example from the THOUGHT TRACK, to show you how to work with it properly. You may think of this as a sort of preliminary to EXERCISE 4.

1. Same as Step 1 in EXERCISE 1.
2. Place the four Aces before you and focus your mind on the number ONE. ONE is the beginning, the vibratory number of CREATIVITY and INDIVIDUALITY. It is the ALPHA: from it all other numbers evolve.
3. Now look at the following excerpt from the THOUGHT TRACK on page 25. This is the SEED PATTERN for the number ONE, as symbolized by the Ace:

   1 = ACE = THE BEGINNING = SPIRIT = FATHER = YOD = INDIVIDUALITY
4. Concentrate on the SEED PATTERN of ONE, repeating it over and over to yourself:

   ONE = THE BEGINNING
   ONE = SPIRIT
   ONE = FATHER
   ONE = YOD (the first Hebrew letter of the Name of God)*
   ONE = INDIVIDUALITY

Soon you will find that your subconscious mind will select one particular SEED from this pattern. It may be ACE = YOD or ACE = INDIVIDUALITY or any of the other SEEDS. This particular SEED will then predominate in your mind whenever you repeat the SEED PATTERN to yourself. However, you may find that your chosen SEED may change from time to time. This is because events in your daily life are constantly changing also. Your Higher Self is aware of this fact, and as you develop your sensitivity, it will direct you to the most appropriate SEED for each occasion.

Before commencing EXERCISE 4, on the THOUGHT TRACK, you should have mastered thoroughly the three previous exercises. You should be able to tune in to the SUIT KEYS at will. Although each numerical sequence is identical, you should be able to link the SEED PATTERN for each number to its individual SUIT KEY, or the material situation implied by that numbered card. For example:

1. ACE OF WANDS = THE BEGINNINGS of ENTERPRISE & DISTINCTION
2. ACE OF CUPS = THE BEGINNING OF LOVE & HAPPINESS
3. ACE OF SWORDS = THE BEGINNING OF STRUGGLE & ANIMOSITY
4. ACE OF PENTACLES = THE BEGINNING OF MONEY INTERESTS

Now go on to EXERCISE 4 on page 25.

*This will be explained further in Chapter 5.

THOUGHT TRACK

Card No.	Seed No. 1	Seed No. 2	Seed No. 3	Seed No. 4	Seed No. 5
1 (Ace)	The beginning	Spirit	Father	Yod	Individuality
2	Form	Fertility	Unexpressed creativity	He	Cooperation
3	Seed	Life	Result, Birth	Vau	Self-expression
4	Foundation	Earth	Solid	Yod	Discipline
5	Uncertainty	Change	Activity	He	Freedom
6	Equilibrium	Stability	Marriage of mind & spirit	Vau	Harmony
7	Soul development	Spiritual perfection	Completion of cycle	Yod	Wisdom, Inner Self
8	Earthly progress	Judgement	Regeneration	He	Executive power & ability
9	Attainment of man	Accumulation	Experience	Vau	Universality, Completion
10	Ultimate result of forces, good & bad	Old cycle complete; New cycle commence	Transition from one suit to another	He	Individuality with purpose
KING	Man	Positive	Active	Yod	Creative
QUEEN	Woman	Negative	Passive	He	Emotional, Responsive
KNIGHT	Young man	Opposition between K&O	Transition	Vau	Struggle, Conflict
PAGE	Boy, Girl, Child	Neutral	Messenger	He	Variable applicable to all

CHART 3

EXERCISE 4: THOUGHT TRACK

1. Same as Step 1 in EXERCISE 1.
2. Select four Minor Arcana cards of the same number; e.g., four THREES, four FOURS, four NINES,etc.
3. Place the four cards before you and repeat slowly and firmly the SEED PATTERN for each card, as listed in the THOUGHT TRACK.
4. Repeat until your subconscious has selected a SEED from the SEED PATTERN for each card.
5. Then concentrate on the four SEEDS you have selected and repeat them slowly and with great emphasis.
6. Relax and allow your inner sensitivity to take over. Continue to concentrate on the SEED PATTERNS and their dominant SEEDS until each one of the SEEDS appears to blend harmoniously with its appropriate SUIT KEY. For example:

THREE	OF WANDS =	LIFE OF ENTERPRISE	& DISTINCTION
(No.)	(Suit)	(Seed No. 2)	(Suit Key)

7. Continue to repeat this association until you feel that the four SEEDS have all taken root in your subconscious, firmly associated with their four SUIT KEYS.

Continue to practice this exercise until you have gone through the entire deck for each suit from Ace through Ten. (Don't worry about the Court Cards at this point; we will discuss them in Chapter 3.) When you feel that you have mastered EXERCISE 4, proceed to EXERCISE 5, which will help to fix these associations firmly in your Higher Mind.

EXERCISE 5: SYNTHESIZING THE SEED WITH THE SUIT KEY

1. Same as Step 1 in EXERCISE 1.
2. Place four cards of the same number before you.
3. Pick up one of the cards and gaze into the picture, repeating the SEED chosen from the SEED PATTERN for that card. Sense the depth of the symbol as you repeat the SEED to yourself; go deeply into it.
4. Bring the card up to your Inner Eye, focusing your energies constantly on the SEED.
5. Imagine the SEED centered in the Inner Eye; then let your mind begin to surround the SEED with the vibratory force of the appropriate SUIT KEY. Allow these vibrations to merge together—*see* them merging in your mind—and hold this fusion steady in your Inner Eye.
6. As the two energies combine and fuse together, allow this new synthesis of force to flow into your subconscious; feel it lifting your thought higher and higher.

7. Holding the inner vision, bring down the card to the Solar Plexus, and as it makes contact with this spiritual area, feel your inner vision expand and prepare to receive new insight as the combined energies touch upon your spiritual center.
8. Repeat Steps 3-7 with each of the four cards.

To make certain you understand this exercise (as it is a very important one), suppose you chose four FIVES, and the first card you picked up was the FIVE OF CUPS. Let's further suppose you had chosen SEED No. 2 for this card. You would then be combining the energies of CHANGE with the SUIT KEY of LOVE & HAPPINESS, or concentrating on

A CHANGE OF LOVE & HAPPINESS

Each card requires the same amount of study. Allot one study period a day to learn four identical numbers from each suit. For example:

Monday = Four ACES
Tuesday = Four TWOS
Wednesday = Four THREES

And so on. Using this system, you will have mastered a basic sensitivity to all ten numbers in just ten days, and will have prepared a satisfactory foundation to advance further. Building a rhythm with your study periods is also important: try to study at theeaoe time every day. Also, let me re-emphasize that the constant handling of the deck will contribute greatly to your progress by continually recharging it with your personal vibrations.

Summing Up the Minor Arcana

The Minor Arcana are divided into four suits of ten cards each:

WANDS
CUPS
SWORDS
PENTACLES

In a spread, a predominance of any one suit provides a general association over and above the individual interpretations. This association is known as the SUIT KEY. The four SUIT KEYS are:

WANDS =ENTERPRISE & DISTINCTION
CUPS = LOVE & HAPPINESS
SWORDS = STRUGGLE & ANIMOSITY
PENTACLES = MONEY INTERESTS

Each unit has an ACE, which equates with the number ONE. Aces represent THE BEGINNING:

1. Seen or unseen
2. Known or unknown
3. Good or bad

Each number has a SEED PATTERN composed of five SEEDS. By concentrating on the SEED PATTERN, you can isolate the SEED that is most meaningful to you for each number and combine it esoterically with the appropriate SUIT KEY.

CHAPTER 3
LEARNING THE COURT CARDS

As with our study of the Aces and the other cards of the Minor Arcana, it is essential that you approach the study of the Court Cards with a relaxed, open attitude, prepared to erase your everyday problems from your mind and concentrate fully on the cards and their messages to you. Make certain that your study periods occur at a time and place where you will not be distracted or interrupted; the further you progress in your study of the Tarot, the more fully you will need to concentrate, to still the normal thinking pattern and allow your subconscious energies to flow freely and enlighten your sensitivities still further.

Sixteen Personalities

Students sometimes become confused when beginning a study of the Court Cards; this is probably because the Court Cards represent *human beings* primarily, and the first impression is a confused jumble of 16 different personalities. These personalities seem to merge together subtly and are hard to clarify if considered individually. So, let's try and simplify the approach to the Court Cards by dividing them into COURT CARD FAMILIES:

1. Each family consists of four members:
   KING
   QUEEN
   KNIGHT
   PAGE
2. Like humanity, the four families are divided into two main types: FAIR and DARK.
   WANDS & CUPS = FAIR HAIR & SKIN
   SWORDS & PENTACLES = DARK HAIR & SKIN

3. All four members of each Court Family have the same physical characteristics:
   WANDS = FAIR HAIR/RED HAIR BLUE EYES FAIR SKIN
   CUPS = LIGHT TO MEDIUM BROWN HAIR/HAZEL EYES MEDIUM SKIN
   SWORDS = DARK BROWN TO BLACK HAIR DARK EYES OLIVE SKIN
   PENTACLES = WHITE HAIR ANY COLOR EYES FAIR SKIN

(Can also represent MEMBERS OF THE DARK-SKINNED RACES.)

Note that if a person has changed the color of his or her hair, it is advisable to identify this person with a Court Card that reflects the change, as this is an obvious expression of an important change in life-style.

We also find that the four members of each family allegorically represent the YOUTH and MATURITY of each human being:

KING = MATURE MAN
QUEEN = MATURE WOMAN
KNIGHT = YOUNG MAN
PAGE = YOUNG BOY/YOUNG GIRL/CHILD OF EITHER SEX

EXERCISE 6: SENSITIVITY TO COURT CARDS

1. Extract all 16 Court Cards from your pack.
2. Separate them into the four COURT FAMILIES.
3. Lay the Court Family of WANDS before you from right to left: KING QUEEN KNIGHT PAGE.
4. Touch the four cards lightly with your fingertips and feel the general characteristics of the WAND FAMILY:
   a. Hair coloring
   b. Eyes
   c. Skin coloring
   d. Overall physical characteristics
5. When you have the general feeling of the WAND FAMILY, try to enlarge and deepen your impressions. Repeat Steps 4a, b and c, this time trying to feel *more depth:*
   a. As you gently touch the four cards, envision the *personality* behind the picture. Start with the KING: see the length of his hair, notice how it is styled. Is it thick, strong hair or is it thin and weak? Is it curly or is it straight? Light or dark?
   b. Concentrate on the KING's eyes. Are they sincere? Does he look kind or stern? Do you feel that you would like to know him?

c. Remember the SUIT KEY for WANDS—ENTERPRISE & DISTINCTION. Does the KING give the impression of worldliness and sophistication? Is he a professional man? Do you think him distinguished? Would you go to him with a problem? Can you feel ENTERPRISE & DISTINCTION when you concentrate on him?

6. Continue the exercise by applying Steps 5a, b and c above to each of the remaining members of the WAND FAMILY: QUEEN, KNIGHT, PAGE.

From this exercise you can see that merely learning the hair, eyes and skin coloring of each Court Card is not enough. Without a deeper insight into their personalities, they lack sufficient individuality for our purposes. Although similar in many ways, sharing a likeness just as any family would, each is different in age and general attitude. Also, the sexes vary: the King and Knight are, of course, male and the Queen female, but remember that the Page can be either sex, representing a young boy or girl or an infant.

The real secret of learning the Court Cards is to treat them like real people. Get to know them as individuals, not merely as pictorial representations of people or as symbols for various human characteristics. Take the time to become thoroughly familiar with each member of each Family, until they are like old friends. Then, each time you meet someone, decide mentally which member of the Court Families this person most resembles. But remember to make these comparisons *in depth* whenever possible, as we often meet people who remind us of other people we already know. This is an excellent exercise, and will help to fix the members of the Court Families more firmly in your subconscious. Be flexible in your comparisons of people to the Court Cards, for humanity does not conform to strict patterns. The cards cannot represent every single type of person on earth, but you will find that the great majority of humanity can be encompassed in these 16 personalities.

Remember that two of the Families, WANDS and PENTACLES, can each represent *two* types of people:

WANDS	= FAIR HAIR	FAIR SKIN	BLUE EYES or
	= RED HAIR	FAIR SKIN	BLUE EYES
PENTACLES	= WHITE HAIR	FAIR SKIN	ANY COLOR EYES or
	= DARK HAIR	DARK SKIN	DARK EYES

So, as you practice your sensitivity exercise, try to envision another addition to the family with the secondary characteristics. For example, think of a family of one type gathered together in a living room, when in walks a cousin of the family with many similarities but different coloring. In the case of PENTACLES, this "cousin" may even be of a different race. It is important to note here that although the personalities depicted in the Court

Families are Caucasian in appearance, members of all races are intended to be represented, just as the ancient masters meant for the esoteric wisdom of the Tarot to pass into the hands of all men, regardless of color or nationality.

As you proceed in your study of the Court Families, remember to link their characteristics firmly with their respective SUIT KEYS (EXERCISE 6, Step 5c):

FAMILY SUIT	CHARACTERISTICS	SUIT KEY
WANDS	FAIR HAIR BLUE EYES FAIR SKIN	ENTERPRISE & DISTINCTION
CUPS	LIGHT/MED. BROWN HAIR HAZEL EYES MED. SKIN	LOVE & HAPPINESS
SWORDS	BROWN/BLACK HAIR DARK EYES OLIVE SKIN	STRUGGLE & ANIMOSITY
PENTACLES	WHITE/DARK HAIR ANY COLOR EYES FAIR/DARK SKIN	MONEY INTERESTS

Studying the Court Families in Depth

Now take the four members of the WANDS Court Family and lay them out before you. This will aid you in implanting the following information firmly in your subconscious. You are now ready to absorb in-depth information about each card and what it represents in a spread with regard to your client, yourself and other persons involved.

WANDS

KING This man is usually married, with a family. He can be secure in his business ventures, perhaps a professional man. His temperament is apt to be hasty at times.

QUEEN This woman is usually married, with a family. She loves her domestic environment and enjoys motherhood. She has an attractive personality which draws people to her.

KNIGHT This young man is apt to be impetuous. He can be found in any walk of life. Sometimes he makes sudden decisions and acts quickly once he decides.

PAGE This boy, girl, or child of either sex is ALWAYS associated with MESSAGES, NEWS, INFORMATION, etc. The source of the information is usually a close friend or relative.

Before you move on to the next Family, spend an evening studying the WANDS, getting to feel more and more at home with them. Think of them as a family that has just moved in next door. They have invited you over for an evening to get acquainted. It takes time to get to know your neighbors properly, so don't be in a hurry. Enjoy the time you spend with them, realize that they will be a part of your life from now on.

CUPS

KING This man is usually a reliable type, possibly associated with Law or Divinity. He can be a bachelor and may be interested in the arts and sciences. He does not object to taking on extra responsibilities.

QUEEN This woman is usually a good wife and mother. She is quite intuitive and sensitive. She can always look on the bright side of things and plans ahead for the future.

KNIGHT This young man is intelligent and can be a romantic. He has many talents and tends to be artistic. He often brings new ideas, invitations and proposals.

PAGE This boy/girl/child of either sex is ALWAYS associated with MESSAGES, NEWS, INFORMATION, etc., like the Page of Wands. This person has a quiet and gentle personality.

SWORDS

KING This man is usually a man of authority, either civilian or attached to the military. His self image is secure, and he could also be with the government or a lawyer. He is level-headed and gives good advice.

QUEEN This woman is usually endowed with a strong character and displays a good wit. Her appearance and mannerisms suggest she has money. She could be a widow or a woman without children.

KNIGHT This young man is always helpful and will give strength to others. He can be a bit too domineering, but always means well. He is very helpful and can be depended upon.

PAGE This boy/girl/child of either sex is ALWAYS associated with MESSAGES, NEWS, INFORMATION, etc., as are the Pages of Wands and Cups. This person is bright and energetic.

PENTACLES

KING This man is usually at the top in industry; he may be associated with mathematics in some way. He is often married, with children, and is living a secure life.

QUEEN This woman is usually efficient, generally very capable at anything she attempts. She can be both mother and business executive. She uses her talents in many ways and can be very creative. However, she tends to be moody, melancholy and sentimental.

KNIGHT This young man is serious and methodical. He is very trustworthy but also can be very unimaginative. He is patient and forebearing and loves animals and nature.

PAGE This boy/girl/child of either sex is ALWAYS associated with MESSAGES, NEWS, INFORMATION, etc., like the Pages of the other three Families. This person respects others and appreciates the value of study and learning.

Multiple Court Cards

Whenever three Court Cards of the same *title* (three Kings, three Pages, etc.) appear in a spread, the following special meanings may apply:

THREE KINGS Can indicate some public recognition, honor, publicity or celebration.

THREE QUEENS Can indicate a meeting, gathering or public function for women.

THREE KNIGHTS Can indicate situations involving schools, colleges, fraternities or other institutions of learning.

THREE PAGES Can indicate important news, information, etc., that will have a strong influence on the client's future activities.

When you have spent an evening getting to know each of the Court Families and feel that you know them well, you may go on to EXERCISE 7, which will deepen the relationship.

EXERCISE 7: COURT CARDS ON THE THOUGHT TRACK

1. Same as Step 1 in EXERCISE 1.
2. Select the SEED from the SEED PATTERN for all KINGS.
3. Pick up one of the KINGS and gaze into the picture, repeating the esoteric SEED chosen from the SEED PATTERN. Experience the depth of all the KING'S characteristics as you continue to repeat the SEED. Go deeply into the nature of the KING.
4. Bring the card to your Inner Eye, focusing your energies on the KING and his SEED.
5. Holding the SEED centered in the Inner Eye, let your mind begin to surround the SEED with the vibratory force of the SUIT KEY. Allow the energies to merge together in your mind.
6. Now holding the SEED and SUIT KEY as one, *feel* the personality of the KING come to life. Remember these concepts, as you meditate:
   a. The SEED = the SOUL
   b. The SUIT KEY = the BODY
   c. The fusing of the two energies brings about the full force of the KING'S nature, transforming him into a complete, substantial personality.
7. Holding this full inner picture of the KING, bring the card down to your Solar Plexus. As it makes contact, become aware of the life and force emanating from the KING.
8. As your concentration gently fades away, replace the first KING with the second and repeat the exercise with each of the remaining three KINGS.
9. After a short rest period, repeat Steps 1-7 with each of the remaining Court Cards.

With frequent practice, this exercise should give you a deep and wonderful familiarity with all the Court Cards and the depths of character they represent.

The Court Cards in Divination

It is important to remember that the Court Cards can represent TWO channels of information in a spread: PEOPLE and SITUATIONS involving people. Your sensitivity and awareness during a divination will indicate the choice. Your client's original question and the nature of the guidance from the spread in general will determine the purpose of each Court Card. An abundance of Court Cards in a spread will indicate that many people are involved in the given situation.

When a Court Card appears as the LAST card in a Celtic Spread,* it indicates that the answer to the client's question or the solution to his problem is strongly connected to a person with the characteristics exemplified by that card. This final Court Card can represent

1. The client
2. A person involved in the client's lifepath
3. A person who MAY become involved with the client in the future.

If you believe that the card represents your client, it may mean that the answer or solution he is seeking rests with this person alone.

There are two significant ways of approaching the Tarot for divination:

1. Ask a direct question and transfer the vibrations from the client to the deck by asking him or her to write down the question.
2. Ask NO questions, but open your consciousness and ask for the WISDOM OF THE TAROT.

When the Wisdom of the Tarot is asked for a female client, and a multiple of QUEENS appear in the spread, they may indicate the different aspects of character displayed by the client in her everyday life. Likewise, if a multiple of KINGS appear in the spread of a male client, this also indicates the various aspects of his character.

Summing Up the Court Cards

Try not to be too rigid or too loose in your interpretation of the Court Cards. If a person seems to strongly resemble the King of Wands, don't hesitate if he doesn't happen to have blue eyes! If you have applied yourself diligently to the Thought Track so far, you will have the knowledge within you to make the right decisions. Before proceeding to a study of the Minor Mentors in the next section, be sure you are thoroughly at home with the Court Cards and have done all the exercises faithfully for a period of at least several weeks. The ability to fuse the proper SEED with the proper SUIT KEY for each card will give you a depth and fluidity in your inner vision.

* The Celtic Spread is a certain way of laying out the cards; we will study it in detail in Chapter 11.

CHAPTER 4
LEARNING THE MAJOR ARCANA

As we learned earlier, the Major Arcana form a separate pack from the Minor Arcana. Twenty-two pictorial cards make up the Major Arcana, each highly symbolic of different states and conditions of man's spiritual life. Just as the Minor Arcana refer to man's body and his mundane experiences, so the Major Arcana deal with his immortal soul and its journey through eternity.

Extract the 22 Major Arcana cards from your Tarot pack and place them in numerical order from 0 (The Fool) through 21 (The World). They should be in the following order:

0 THE FOOL
1 THE MAGICIAN
2 THE HIGH PRIESTESS
3 THE EMPRESS
4 THE EMPEROR
5 THE HIEROPHANT
6 THE LOVERS
7 THE CHARIOT
8 STRENGTH
9 THE HERMIT
10 WHEEL OF FORTUNE
11 JUSTICE
12 THE HANGED MAN
13 DEATH
14 TEMPERANCE
15 THE DEVIL
16 THE TOWER
17 THE STAR
18 THE MOON
19 THE SUN
20 JUDGEMENT
21 THE WORLD

Our goal is not to try to learn all the individual symbology contained in the Major Arcana, for each Tarot Master and the artist working with him endeavors to include all that he considers significant in interpreting each card, but we will strive to understand the symbology before us in the Rider Waite Deck, which I have found to be the clearest and most profound to work with.

The Major Arcana contain the mysteries of the soul and its purpose here on earth. Each card can open vast dimensions of spirituality to you if you study it with diligence and purity of purpose. Together, these 22 cards will take you into realms of higher consciousness and reveal vistas of esoteric knowledge that remain veiled to those who choose the more mundane paths of life.

Since we are dealing with spiritual aspects here, the proper way to approach the study of the Major Arcana each day is with prayer. The Daily Prayer will uplift your thoughts to a higher level and open the gateway to the peace and comfort that come with a spiritual kinship to the Tarot. Our next exercise, therefore, is this Daily Prayer as applied specifically to each of the 22 cards.

EXERCISE 8: DAILY PRAYER WITH THE MAJOR ARCANA

1. Same as Step 1 in EXERCISE 1.
2. Say each prayer slowly and thoughtfully, with the appropriate card before you. Look at the picture and become totally involved with the symbols portrayed, for the picture is you — your Higher Self. Begin with the unnumbered card, THE FOOL:

0 THE FOOL

Dear Heavenly Father, through Thy divine grace let me feel the Holy Spirit within me. Grant me the innocence of the Fool,help me to let go of earthly fears and walk in peace with Thee this day. Let my ears listen only to Thy higher wisdom. Let me walk freely, knowing that I am protected in Thy love. I long for the innocent faith of a child, and because I am a child of God, I know it to be my birthright. As I walk into this new day I pray that I shall always be aware of Thy holy presence. I know that only fear separates me from the comfort of Thy define love. This day I will try to express my love for Thee, dear Father, in all I do and say. I will rid myself of fear, which is the shadow of man, and with Thy holy blessing, walk in heavenly light. Amen.

1 THE MAGICIAN

This day, dear Lord, my needs weigh heavy, filling my heart and mind with apprehension. There is so much I want to accomplish and I am in need of Thy divine strength. I know that all I have to do is to reach out and let Thy love permeate my whole being, and all is mine. If I forget, dear Father, let me feel the comfort of Thy everlasting love, let me recognize Thee in everyone I see today. When I am called upon to make decisions that affect not only myself but others, let me first come to Thee for heavenly reassurance. May I ever be conscious that success is only of this earth and that all I do should be with Thee in mind. Thou art ever with me, in every decision, every hope, every hurt. I pray that Thy presence bless all I do today. Amen.

2 THE HIGH PRIESTESS

Bless me, dear Father, and let me understand all that is happening in my life today. I ask for the Christ Light to shine on all my dark corners so that I may look upon the problems that will confront me. I pray for the gentleness of saints and to learn that no matter how much I feel right, there is always another side to consider. Teach me humility, which is true strength, and let my thoughts and actions today be constructive and helpful. Grant me the ability to help someone in need and lighten a shadow in his life as I ask Thee for the same gift. Teach me consideration and help me to shift the concern I have for myself to others more in need. Take from me the fear of losing my image in the eyes of others. In Thy sweet mercy, let those who love me know me as I really am. All this, dear Father, I ask in Thy Holy Name. Amen.

3 THE EMPRESS

How can I thank Thee, dear Lord, for the many blessings of love and life that surround me? May I ever be aware of Thy blessings as I approach this new day. Let me fill my heart and soul with fresh hope, let the love that passeth all understanding be mine this day. I pray for the fullness of Thy mercy to relieve me of my anxieties. I give thanks for all my loved ones and I pray that I will have the strength to let them know today how much I am blessed by their love and concern for my well being. I am a child of God, I am well blessed, and this day I will feel abundant with the love of God and my dear ones. The light that I feel in this prayer I will carry as a living flame within me. I pray that all those I meet today will share the warmth that is mine and feel the strength of this beautiful blessing. Amen.

4 THE EMPEROR

I offer this day to Thee, dear Father, for I know I will need the companionship of the Holy Spirit. I need Thee by my side when I am confronted with my daily tasks. In Thy loving wisdom allow me to see things as they really are, to recognize authority and leadership and respect the rights and duties of others. Alert my mind so that I may give my best to the work I have to accomplish. Open my selfish mind and let me be receptive to the ideas and needs of others. For in recognizing their needs, I know I am recognizing Thee. Grant me peace this day; Thy will, not mine, be done. Amen.

5 THE HIEROPHANT

Release me, dear Father, from the bonds of pride. Help me to understand that others, too, have a point of view. Teach me to listen and not be critical of the thoughts and actions of my fellow men. Expand my tolerance so that I may help those who may be searching. My vision of life often becomes focused only on my personal needs and desires. With Thy almighty blessing I pray that this day I can truly give myself and not be concerned about my own welfare and feelings. Relieve me of my narrow scope of thinking, release me from my ego, and in Thy love let my actions be a worthwhile acknowledgement that Thou, dear Father, liveth in me this day forevermore. Amen.

6 THE LOVERS

This day I pray for tranquility in the many duties I have to perform. I ask that I may hear the voice of truth within me. I have before me many choices to make and I ask that no matter how small they may be, I will always be ready and willing to receive Thy holy guidance and wisdom. Temptations are many, dear Father, and it can be so easy not to care. I need Thee in my daily life, I am tired of being careless and drifting with the crowd. Give me the strength to do what is right, walk with me this day, and I will do my best to fill it with joy and perfection. Protect me, dear Father, from all my fears and any wrongdoing; fill me with the Holy Spirit and leave no room for any unkind thoughts or irresponsible actions. Amen.

7 THE CHARIOT

Today I must be in control of all my emotions, they must not injure anyone or lead me to injure myself. Dear Lord, my life is so full of problems. So often I go from day to day trying to ignore their many consequences. I pray for heavenly forces to rejuvenate me and fill my whole being with divine strength so that I may be in control of everything I say and do. Insecurity clouds my vision, the love and respect I yearn for from others is spoiled by my childish demand for unnecessary attention. I think and say things that I am truly sorry for, I hesitate to make apologies, for even that I do not feel capable of doing right. I am too concerned with myself and ask Thee, dear Father, to release me from the prison of false ego that I have built around myself. Fortify me with strength of character and let me direct my energies into making others happy. I ask this in all humility. Amen.

8 STRENGTH

Fill my day, dear Lord, with the strength to resist all that may offend Thee. Too often do I resort to my inner weaknesses. Teach me the beauty of inner strength, to know the difference between selfishness and charitable actions. If it be Thy holy will, let me use my strength to help others. Allow me to be a fortress for those who seek comfort and solace. If today I am tempted to use my strength solely for my own purpose and pleasure, remind me and show me where my strength can best be used. Help me to use gentleness when I feel the need to force my opinions on others; grant me the patience to wait instead of pushing. I pray for true strength of character and long for the stillness of my material wants. Grant me the grace of knowing that true strength is faith in Thee. Amen.

9 THE HERMIT

In my loneliness I cry out to Thee, dear Father. So often I feel neglected and unappreciated. My life lacks joy and I come to Thee seeking the comfort of divine love. In my despair, each bright morning is clouded with my tears. I long for the light of understanding to brighten my daily life. Too often I am content in this misery and tell myself that no one cares, but my heart knows better. Help me, Father, to raise my head and see the light of truth. Sometimes I am ashamed to ask Thee again for Thy forgiveness, So I continue in my miserable ways. I know this is not the truth, I know Thy mercy is everlasting. Before I experience the day ahead, help me to raise my face to Thee. Let Thy light shine upon me, fill my soul with new hope and erase the misery of self pity. I reach out my hand, dear Father, and feel thy blessing now filling me with the heavenly light of new hope and happiness. With this holy light bright within me I can now face the shadows of my own actions. I give Thee my fears of yesterday as I look up at the eternal light of love and truth. Amen.

10 THE WHEEL

My love for Thee, dear Father, is so inconstant, it seems easy to appreciate my blessings when all is well with me. Grant me the courage to reach out into the dark of my own misdemeanors. Life is ever changing, and I need the wisdom to understand the seasons of my life. Help me to understand how to accept these changes, for I am weak and sometimes feel that I don't know how to cope. I feel insecure and long for love and yet it seems that I continually struggle and try to do it on my own. I turn to Thee, dear Father, as I approach this new day. Fill me with faith and trust in the almighty mercy of Thy love. Teach me to accept whatever the day may bring, and if it be pain or hurt, to accept it graciously, knowing that Thou wilt take it from me if the burden is too heavy. Teach me to pray and retain the courage Thou placeth within me. Amen.

11 JUSTICE

The labors of yesterday will be justified in this new day. I am weak, dear Father, and afraid of the consequences of my own actions. It is terrible to know fear and allow it to blind me to Thy mercy. I need Thee by my side to face any justice bestowed upon me. When others judge me, open my eyes and let me understand the reasons why. Help me not to be quick to judge the acts of others. May I represent kindness and mercy when others condemn. When this night falls, may the love and understanding I show today give another soul comfort and happiness. As I start this new day, may this prayer rest in my heart and find its way to thee. Amen.

12 THE HANGED MAN

Faith has been the strength of saints and can withstand all cruel reasoning. The simplicity of faith is my need for today. Grant me this gift, dear Lord: When things go wrong, let me have faith; when I am challenged, let me show faith; when I seek for answers, let me ask in faith. I put my day into Thy divine order, I ask Thee to be a part of all I do today. Let faith shine through my eyes so that others in need of faith may share it. I will not demand answers today, I will not be concerned, for my faith is in Thee. I offer my day to all who are in need of Thy word. Let this day be an example to all and a worthwhile offering to my heavenly Father. Amen.

13 DEATH

I am a part of Thy eternal plan and know that change is hard for me to understand. Because I am insecure, I try to hold on to that which gives me strength. Help me to understand this ever-changing existence. When change is thrust upon me, fill me with understanding and acceptance. Life moves on and nothing is permanent in this world; this I know, dear Father, but I have not always the strength to recognize thy Holy will. Open my eyes so that I may see and understand the reasons for change and be ready to accept them in my daily life. I offer this day to you, dear Lord, and as the day begins, prepare me to see and acknowledge the constant change in everything. When change comes into my life, be with me, Father, so that I may find the comfort of Thy holy presence and accept Thy divine will. Amen.

14 TEMPERANCE

Today I pray for total balance in every thought, word and deed. Help me, Father, to maintain this perfect balance; let no one upset the peace I find here with Thee this morning. Tranquility and peace are the result of temperance, and I pray for this total harmony in all that I may do this day. Speak my heart, dear Lord, and let me know if my actions offend thee. Purify my thoughts so that I do no one an injustice. Let the beauty of all Thy gifts to men inspire my soul, and may this day be filled and made complete by a contribution from me. Peace, tranquility, balance, harmony. Amen.

15 THE DEVIL

As I begin this day with Thee, dear Father, I realize that my way of life can take me away from Thee. My earthly pleasures and material concerns often blind me to Thy gift of life. Teach me to appreciate all that I have and not to spoil my day with greed for things that really do not matter. Teach me a sense of true values, fill me with the treasures of Heaven. I pray for all my needs and for the needs of my loved ones, and may I spend this day thanking Thee for all the blessings Thou hast given to me and my family. My worries and concerns of this earthly life I now offer up to Thee so that I may walk in peace this day. Amen.

16 THE TOWER

I have lost sight of myself, dear Lord; I feel that I have wandered far away from Thy heavenly love. I have been too concerned with myself and in my selfishness I forget to pray for those I love. Break down this facade, dear Father, and let me truly know myself. I am lost and full of false pride; take me unto Thy loving care, open my eyes and let me see the glory of truth. I feel afraid to let go and yet my need to return to Thee is much greater. Help me, Father, to come home and bless this new day with new life and hope. Let me start living again today. Amen.

17 THE STAR

I thank Thee, heavenly Father, for all Thy wondrous gifts: for the blessing of health Thou so generously bestoweth upon me; for my loved ones and the responsibilities I have toward them. Thank you, Father, for my home, and all my humble possessions. It is good to feel the life energies surging through my body and to know that I am a part of Thy Divine Plan. As I face this new day, let me be aware of all the blessings that surround me; may I take time to look at the flowers and to see Thy purpose in every little child. How merciful Thou art, dear Father, to be always with me, and each breath I take should be a constant reminder of Thy presence. How often I go through my day without speaking to Thee. Only when I am miserable and unhappy do I seem to acknowledge Thee. Let me take the time to count my blessings, and in the joy of this new day to thank Thee with my whole heart and soul. My every hope and desire is to know Thee better; please show me how. Amen.

18 THE MOON

So often I am deceived, dear Lord, by my own actions and thoughts. I become so totally involved in my own schemes that I lose contact with reality. My imagination builds a dividing wall and I painfully try to live in my own false world. Break down my fears and let me feel the healing of Christ. I feel so cut off, dear Father, help me to find my way back to Thee. Teach me to pray and relieve me of all my past sins. May this new day bring me the closeness I need so much. Help me to forgive myself so that I may come to Thee; show me the way of Christ and let His light shine upon me. Give me the strength to leave my old ways and start this day with Thee, dear Father. If I should weaken, let me hear Thy voice. I need Thy guidance, I need to see the light; in Thy mercy grant me this peace. Amen.

19 THE SUN

Today I want to share my happiness with you, dear Father, as so often I forget to do this. Every simple pleasure I experience I want to share with Thee. When I look around me and see the many blessings and achievements that my family and I have received, my heart fills with indescribable joy. How can I thank Thee, dear Father? The blessings are so many. Let me give this day to Thee in love and adoration; may all those who share this day with me feel Thy gracious spirit at work, at home and in everything I do and experience. May all the decisions I make be worthy of Thy continued blessings. I am so full of love that it is difficult for me to express my true feelings. My faith is strengthened when I see all my blessings around me. My prayer today is to express my appreciation by giving others the joy that the Christ Light brings. Amen.

20 JUDGEMENT

Thank you, Father, for the awakening I feel inside me; how fortunate I am to be a child of God. Thou hast known my torment and struggle, and when I was in the darkness of despondency Thou did show me the way. How grateful I am to know Thy love; in Christ all things are possible. There is so much that I must learn and accomplish; help me to completely restore my soul with Thy bounteous love. Fill me with Thy heavenly grace so that I may lift my consciousness to a higher level of understanding. I am blessed with the faith of knowing my Father and I wish to walk the way of Christ. If it be Thy holy will, let me help others who are searching for Thy blessed presence. May this day be filled with continued joy of the spirit; how glad I am to be alive! May every thought and action glorify thy Holy Name. Amen.

21 THE WORLD

Release me, Father, from my insecurity, help me to do what I must do this day. Liberate me from the limitations of my own thoughts. May I be generous in my opinions and allow for the success of others. Let me face any changes with courage and understanding. Grant me the grace to see that change is a new experience I must accept in order to grow spiritually. Take away any fear I may have and replace it with the courage to see and acknowledge the changing world and how I must grow with it. I thank Thee for Thy many blessings and ask Thee, dear Father, to give me Thy special blessing today on all that I may do. I pray for confidence and guidance, and in all humility I accept whatever responsibility may be given me. Stay with me, dear Father, and share this special day with me. Amen.

Within this treasure chest of human emotion, you will discover a prayer appropriate for each day of your life. The beautiful vibrations radiated by each Major symbol will help you to commune with God and bring His light into your mind and heart whenever you need it. As you become familiar with these prayers, you can add whatever personal appeal you wish, but keep your thoughts simple and direct. Prayer takes us within ourselves and allows us to break down the barriers of materiality that so often separate us from the loving grace of our Heavenly Father.

The Major Arcana Symbols in Our Lives

The secret of learning the Major Arcana is not to see them as individual cards. Rather, think of them as 22 symbols which represent YOU, MANKIND, HUMANITY.

Your approach to learning these symbols should be an intensely personal one — you must strive to find the interpretation that is right for *you*. Don't worry about the interpretations of other writers and Tarot Masters as expressed in the multitude of books on the subject. Rather, using the guidelines I will present here, approach each card with a totally open mind, free from bias and preconceptions. You must learn to look beyond the pictures, the symbols on the cards, and into your own Higher Self, so that the Major Arcana become a part of your consciousness, as natural as breathing. In this way you will open the floodgates for the spiritual fountains of wisdom to flow into your soul and mind.

When you find that a certain symbol promotes a certain association or thought pattern on a regular basis, don't fight it — don't waste time trying to reconcile it with another interpretation you may feel at a more surface level. If you receive a definite impression, follow it through, explore it in depth, and when you feel comfortable with it, make it your own.

Look at your daily life and habits: without thinking much about it consciously, you have adopted a certain way of going about everyday chores, a pattern of behavior. Some may brush their teeth before taking a shower; others, only afterwards. Some people can only sleep lying on their backs, while others have to curl up on their right or left sides. As a rule, we don't give these decisions a second thought — they come as naturally to us as eating.

This is the way to work with the Tarot. Our goal is to get to the point at which we no longer have to think about interpretations or meanings of cards consciously. To enable us to do this, we must come to understand the 22 symbols of the Major Arcana in relation to our own lives. We must become aware of their meaning in our everyday experiences; as we do so, we will come to understand ourselves as well.

As an example of how we come to feel the influence of these symbols in our lives, let me tell you about a recent experience of feeling the EMPRESS vibration in my daily routine. I was at home, busily preparing for a special birthday party. I had fixed lots of wonderful food and the house was looking absolutely perfect. In a short time, all of my family would be arriving for the celebration. I had on a new dress, the sun was shining, I felt rich and blessed with abundance. Then the family arrived, and when the candles were lit on the birthday cake, I looked at all my children and grandchildren and felt intensely the joy and blessings that were showered upon me. It would be impossible to adequately describe the feelings of happiness and contentment I experienced then — except to say that I truly reflected the vibration of THE EMPRESS!

The symbols of the Major Arcana, then, represent every experience that man can encounter on the earth plane. The secret that the ancient masters have handed down to us is that all earthly emotions and experiences are contained within the symbology of the Tarot, and a true and thorough understanding of this symbology enables us to elevate our everyday feelings and experiences into a higher spiritual vibration, transmuting our very lives just as the ancient alchemists transmuted base metals into gold.

The Story of Life

Think of the Major Arcana as a story — the story of life — with 22 chapters. To fully understand the story, you must become involved in and study each chapter thoroughly, not only for itself but also for its relationship to the chapters that precede and follow it. Each card is a separate chapter in the story. Merely knowing the title of each chapter is not enough; you need to understand thoroughly the content of the chapter — the characters and situations involved. This is the only way to fully appreciate what is conveyed in the *whole story.*

The conscious mind is not able to grasp fully the symbolism of the Tarot. You must relax and allow your subconscious to absorb the message contained in the story of the Major Arcana, for it is an extension of the physical into the spiritual — another dimension of comprehension. It cannot be adequately described, for it is built on foundations of the subconscious — its reality is within the Higher Self. Through meditation and a sincere desire to understand the timeless message of the Tarot, we can come to a deep, personal comprehension of our own spiritual framework — who we are, what we have built for ourselves and why, and where we are going.

Our next exercise is designed to help you develop the sensitivity required to attain this spiritual understanding of the Major Arcana symbols. Study it carefully, for the Spiritual Path of the Major Arcana is the story of life — the life of each of us on the earthly plane and beyond.

EXERCISE 9: THE SPIRITUAL PATH OF THE MAJOR ARCANA

1. Same as Step 1 in EXERCISE 1.
2. Read and meditate slowly and carefully on the following story, with the appropriate cards before you as you do so.

0 THE FOOL

We begin our journey with the pure, untouched soul, not yet of this world. All wisdom and knowledge, containing the total essence of God, are contained in the innocence of a newborn baby, physically present in the world now, yet still enveloped in the Higher Consciousness.

1 THE MAGICIAN

Before man are the tools of Higher Consciousness. As he becomes involved with the material plane, he is given all he needs to achieve success here on earth. As he develops his ego, he must endeavor to retain his spiritual equilibrium and use his God-given tools to reach his heavenly goal.

2 THE HIGH PRIESTESS

On the earth plane there are both negative and positive forces, material and spiritual values. Within the HIGH PRIESTESS man can learn to face all that may oppose him in realizing this eternal balance of energies. He must learn to balance his emotions and desires and to direct his thoughts to his Higher Consciousness.

3 THE EMPRESS

Man's blessings are plentiful, God's gifts are abundant. Man must endeavor to acknowledge and give thanks to the source of his rich inheritance. The reward of earthly labor is achieved in Heaven. Man must learn that his status in this world is only temporary, and by the way he conducts his life here is measured the eternal growth of his soul.

4 THE EMPEROR

As man obeys the laws of God, he must also recognize these laws in his fellow man. He who has chosen humility in this life must not envy others. Man must learn to respect leadership and authority, and raising his thoughts to the Supreme Force, must learn to act in a kingly manner, just as an earthly ruler must acknowledge a higher authority.

5 THE HIEROPHANT

The Church of God on earth must prosper, and man must contribute his efforts toward this goal. He must defend openly what he believes and oppose that which offends his conscience. There is only one Truth, and man must live by it, freeing himself from anything that turns him from the will of God.

6 THE LOVERS

As the soul progresses on earth, it is presented with many choices. Man is held responsible for the choices he makes; if difficulty arises, he must listen to his inner voice, which will direct him to higher guidance. His destiny lies before him, but he always has the free will to make his own decisions. As he reaches maturity of mind and body, he must understand that whatever he sows, he will reap.

7 THE CHARIOT

Another lesson to be learned is that of control. Man must adapt himself to the laws of men, as well as to those of God. He must learn to be in command of his emotions and not allow them to rule his life. He must understand that he is a soul with a body, not a body with a soul.

8 STRENGTH

True strength is spiritual, not physical, and man must learn to use this strength of spirit to sustain himself in times of trouble, to lift himself above worldly turmoil. Man must realize that he is never alone with his doubts and fears, and that heavenly comfort can be his if he will only reach up for it.

9 THE HERMIT

As man progresses spiritually, he realizes that God never turns away from him. He is never alone, and his most secret deeds and thoughts cannot be hidden. Therefore, it is important for him to examine his motives carefully. In times of loneliness and despair, when all seems dark, he need only raise his vision to see the Christ Light pointing the way.

10 WHEEL OF FORTUNE

Life is like the Wheel: when man is up, the only way to go is down; when he is down, he can be sure that he will eventually go up again. Nothing in this life is stable and permanent; man must learn to accept the challenges and the blessings, for both are important to his soul's growth.

11 JUSTICE

Justice is the voice of man's conscience. He must learn to obey it, in order to maintain his inner balance. The Higher Consciousness of man directs his actions, and if it is ignored, man loses his spiritual equilibrium. This causes chaos in his life and harm to himself and his loved ones.

12 THE HANGED MAN

In order to progress spiritually, man must curtail his pursuit of material gain. As he develops in maturity, he should take time to reflect on his past life and submit his future to God. It is difficult to change direction when a man has devoted too much of his life to materiality, but it is at this point that he should have the courage to surrender his material needs to the Higher Consciousness and redirect his steps to God.

13 DEATH

Man has made Death another word for fear. But death is not the end — it is transition from one plane of existence to another. Physical death is the rebirth of the soul into another phase of existence on the journey back to God. If man will allow his ego to die on the earthly plane and experience the transformation of his Higher Self, he will lose his fear of bodily death and come to accept it as a natural part of his progression.

14 TEMPERANCE

When man is able to allow his Higher Consciousness to flow freely into his conscious thoughts, he will experience the beauty of order and harmony in his life. He must learn to be moderate in all things in order to maintain this tranquility. The will of God becomes his own will and he sees the glory of God in every living thing.

15 THE DEVIL

During the soul's journey, man must learn to use his powers correctly. He can choose to use them for material gain or in a manner which will increase his spiritual awareness. Temptation will be presented in many forms, but the powerful appeal of evil may always be overcome by reaching out to the Higher Consciousness.

16 THE TOWER

Often man feels the desire to change his ways, but lacks the strength of will to achieve his spiritual goals. He may wish to break down his ego and his materialistic pursuits, but be prevented from doing so by fear. To find peace and contentment, it is sometimes necessary for man to experience loss and tragedy before he can find spiritual comfort and strength.

17 THE STAR

In times of darkest depression, THE STAR radiates the guidance of our Higher Consciousness. Man can overcome all fear if he will follow this light. It is the source of all inner strength and will lead him through the night into the beautiful dawn of supreme understanding.

18 THE MOON

Of all the experiences a man must encounter on the earthly plane, his final test is faith. When he has passed beyond dependence upon reason and resolves to submit his being to the will of God, then he will truly understand the sustaining power of faith.

19 THE SUN

After the soul has undergone the trials of faith, the bonds that tie it to the earthly plane are severed, and man can know true liberation and attainment. The knowledge of the true nature of his being and the part he is playing in the Universal Plan brings him the glorious reward of union with the God within himself.

20 JUDGEMENT

Man can now see the Divine Purpose through his own Higher Consciousness. He leaves behind all that once meant security to him and redirects his life and all his energy toward the glory of God. Life now has meaning for him, and man realizes why he is here. He looks at life with renewed hope and prayer.

21 THE WORLD

The soul goes on and on, gathering experience after experience within God's Universal Plan. One experience gives birth to another throughout the eternal cycle of life and death. Existence is continuous, ever changing but never ending, as the soul of man passes from one form to another. Each life he lives is only a glimpse into eternity, a chance for him to refocus and refine his ideals toward God's will. Each time fear and indecision must be overcome, so that the soul can take one more step upward on the journey back to its eternal Source and in so doing realize that it is a part of God, an immortal manifestation of God's unlimited love.

Keeping a Tarot Log

Before proceeding to EXERCISE 10, you should set up and keep a TAROT LOG for yourself (see p. 56 for example). This is not the same as the DAILY RECORD BOOK (p. 13), which is used for personal readings. The TAROT LOG is specifically to record your impressions and details of meditation on the symbols of the Major Arcana. Immediately upon completing EXERCISE 10, and each time you meditate on the Major Arcana, you should write down all your impressions, in as much detail as possible. This will help to fix them deeply in your subconscious. Meditation is similar to dreaming: we can quickly forget important details if we do not train our minds to remember them. The TAROT LOG will also provide you with a record of your sensitivity progress, which will grow as you study. Take as much time as you need, try to recall as much detail as possible. If you need more room, write on the backs of the sheets or use others. Here are some helpful hints in filling out your log:

1. You may find that some Major symbols are easier to meditate upon than others. Record your impressions of this.
2. Certain colors may appear more brilliant than others. Record this.
3. You may find it easy to go deep within certain symbols, as if walking some distance into the picture. Record this.
4. You may find yourself conversing with the character in the symbol. Record the details of this conversation.
5. You may hear a voice or voices not connected with any one symbol or character. Record what you hear.
6. Upon entering the picture of a card, you may find that the scenery differs from that portrayed. Record what you see.
7. You may be aware of fragrances. Record them.
8. Your sense of touch may be heightened. Describe what you feel and what you touch.
9. You may receive insights and knowledge, either general or relating to a particular subject. Record every detail.

TAROT LOG

MAJOR ARCANA CARD:__________ DATE:____________________

MEDITATION
TIME BEGAN:____________________ FINISHED: ________________

DETAILS OF MEDITATION:

ANALYSIS OF IMPRESSIONS RECEIVED:

CHART 4

EXERCISE 10: ENTERING THE MAJOR ARCANA

1. Same as Step 1 in EXERCISE 1.
2. Select one of the 22 Major Arcana cards and place it before you.
3. Relax your mind and body and focus your attention on the card. Allow your mind to drink in every detail of color and shape.
4. Say the appropriate Prayer of Invocation for your card, as learned in EXERCISE 8.
5. As you recite the prayer, absorb every detail of the card until you feel ready to hold the picture in your Inner Eye. Then close your eyes, bring the card up to your forehead, and recreate the picture in your mind in full detail.
6. Feel the picture in your Inner Eye take on length and depth, like a three-dimensional movie. As the view expands and the borders of the picture recede, gently PUSH yourself forward with your Solar Plexus until you enter the picture, like going through a doorway.
7. As you enter this new dimension, become sensitive to life and movement all around you. Feel yourself become enveloped in this new world which is no longer merely a picture. The figures are no longer still; you are now in the world of the Superconscious and everything and everyone is very real.
8. You are now a part of this world, life is vibrant all around you, colors are bright, everything is moving and real. You can feel the breeze, the grass underfoot, the warmth of the sun. You smell the scent of flowers and look all around you, absorbing all you can.
9. Start to walk and become totally involved in what is happening around you. Listen and hear voices speaking, introduce yourself to the character or characters in the card, converse with them. Treat them as real, living people, but be as natural as possible. Be respectful, but do not be intimidated by their high natures (e.g., THE EMPRESS, THE HIEROPHANT). NOTE: When entering such cards as DEATH, THE DEVIL, THE HANGED MAN, etc., it is important not to be afraid of these figures. Realize that they have their functions to perform in God's Plan, know that God's love and protection is with you and that they cannot harm you in any way.
10. Let the vibrations of this spiritual plane permeate your whole being and feel the rejuvenation of the higher forces.

11. When you become aware that your conscious mind is bringing you back, gently PUSH from your Solar Plexus, keeping your eyes closed, and slowly withdraw from the spiritual world. When you feel yourself back in your original meditating position and the life and movement has faded back into the card, slowly allow the image of the card to disappear from your Inner Eye, like a fade-out in a movie. Allow the sounds and feelings of this world to return to your consciousness before opening your eyes.

12. The meditation is over. Now, before the images fade from your memory, enter your impressions in your TAROT LOG — all the details you can remember, then your analysis of these experiences.

13. Repeat this exercise with each of the 22 Major Arcana cards, until you feel thoroughly familiar with all of them. Don't try to do too many at one time; one or two a day is enough.

Reading with the Major Arcana Only

When the Tarot is used for spiritual guidance, you need use only the Major Arcana. The Minor Arcana concern our mundane activities, so there is no need to include them when spiritual questions are being asked. As you become more sensitive to the cards, you may wish to buy a second Tarot pack and use only the Major Arcana specifically for spiritual readings. If you do choose to use two packs, remember that the second pack must be carefully "seasoned," just as the first was. Once you extract the 22 Major Arcana cards, do not shuffle them with the extra pack of Minor Arcana you will have. Separate them — wrap the 22 cards in their own Tarot cloth and put the remaining 56 cards away. Your second "spiritual pack" should be used for meditation and spiritual practice only. Use the complete pack of your first deck for general spreads and reading.

Summing Up the Major Arcana

The 22 cards of the Major Arcana are symbolic of man's spiritual nature and his soul's journey from life to life as it progresses back to God. The wisdom that can be gained from these cards is of the highest kind, and we must always approach them with the purest and most positive attitudes we can achieve. For this reason, they require much meditation and study, with patience and a sincere and humble desire to learn. The proper prayer should always be recited before studying each card, and a complete TAROT LOG should be kept of each meditation.

SECTION II

CHAPTER 5
UNDERSTANDING THE MINOR MENTORS

In order to help you understand the symbology of the Tarot more thoroughly, I have prepared what I call "Mentors" for each card in the deck. I have broken them down into Mentors for the Minor Arcana, the Court Cards and the Major Arcana, and I suggest that you study them in this order, just we have approached them in previous chapters.*The term "Mentor" means "wise loyal advisor, a teacher or coach." In Greek mythology Mentor was the loyal friend and advisor of Odysseus and the teacher of his son Telemachus.

The purpose of these Tarot Mentors is to bring together in an organized fashion a collection of esoteric knowledge about each of the 78 cards in the deck. I have combined the traditional definitions of meaning for the cards with my own method of interpretation, which I consider helpful to the development of an inner sensitivity to the Tarot. You will also be able to see how each card relates to other occult studies such as Astrology, Gnothology (esoteric Numerology), and to a limited degree, the Cabala. A reproduction of each card is also included, to help fix it visually in your mind while studying the other information, without having to refer to your actual deck. Each Mentor contains the following types of information:

1. KEY
2. REVERSE KEY
3. MEMORIES
4. GUIDELINES
5. COMPARISON CHART
6. DIVINATION IN DEPTH

*You will find the actual Mentors following the introductory chapters, as Chapters 7, 8 and 9.

Key

The KEY is used when the card is in the UPRIGHT position. It is an immediate guide to clarifying the card and its symbol. However, it should be considered merely as an aide in promoting your sensitivity and *not* as the only definition. You cannot rely wholly on the Mentors for interpretation; they should be used only as a guide in developing your own modus operandi.

Reverse Key

When the card is reversed, the interpretation differs. This does not necessarily mean that the interpretation of the card is negative. Learning the REVERSE KEYS should be your goal as soon as you have mastered the upright KEYS. The REVERSE KEY, like the upright key, is intended to stimulate your psychic and spiritual energies — a starting point from which to eventually reach your own individual interpretations.

Memory

This is a simple two-line rhyme for each card, in both upright and reverse positions. If you have difficulty memorizing the KEYS and REVERSE KEYS, you may find it easier to master these little rhymes, which convey the same message as the KEYS and REVERSE KEYS.

Guidelines

Before making full use of the GUIDELINES, it is necessary for you to have thoroughly mastered the preceding lessons and exercises in this Handbook. The GUIDELINES are interpretational possibilities which must be combined with the sensitivity you have developed up to this point. Always go with your intuition, whether the GUIDELINES agree and disagree; but it you have properly developed your inner awareness, your feelings will most often lead you to the correct GUIDELINE for the occasion. Remember that a divination is like reading the story of someone's life. When you feel assured that you can tune into the correct GUIDELINE and find that it fits meaningfully into the picture the cards are disclosing, you have reached the necessary level of sensitivity for divination. Until this level is reached, you should never practice serious divination for another person; to try and guess which GUIDELINE to use is obviously neither moral nor ethical.

Comparison Chart (I)

The COMPARISON CHART is to give the apprentice a glimpse into the more advanced areas of relationships between the Tarot and the other occult sciences. Obviously, any one of these studies is sufficiently complex to fill several volumes by itself — and indeed, many excellent works exist on each subject. There is no shortage of material today, as in former years, as a trip to any occult bookstore will reveal. The Tarot is intimately related to three of the most important occult sciences:

1. THE CABALA (including the Tetragrammaton)
2. ASTROLOGY
3. GNOTHOLOGY (Esoteric Numerology)

The COMPARISON CHART will present a key relationship with each of these sciences for each card. This is merely for your information, and the complete absorption of this knowledge is not crucial at this point in your studies, but it will help to broaden and deepen your feeling for the cards on a subconscious level as you study the Mentors, and so should not be overlooked. You will find that each COMPARISON CHART is divided into four parts, corresponding to the four characters of the TETRAGRAMMATON, the ancient Hebrew name for God: YOD HE VAU HE. Before we can proceed further with an explanation of the COMPARISON CHART, it is necessary for us to take a side trip and learn something about this sacred and mysterious word.

The Tetragrammaton

According to the traditional beliefs of the Hebrews and of the Cabala, the Tetragrammaton is too sacred to be spoken aloud; a legend says that anyone who discovers the correct pronunciation of the Sacred Name will have the key to all knowledge. But the Hebrew language has no vowels, so it is very difficult to be certain of the exact pronunciation of any word as originally intended thousands of years ago. Therefore, you will find a number of different transliterations from the Hebrew characters of the Name:

JHVH JHWH YHVH IHVH

In modern usage, these characters are rendered as JEHOVAH or YAHWEH. In the Hebrew texts we find the words ADONAI or ELOHIM (Gods) substituted whenever the Name of God is referred to. It is said that the Name was unknown to man until God gave it to Moses in the wilderness. Since that time, it has become lost through the wickedness of man, and the correct pronunciation will only be revealed at the coming of the true Messiah.

According to the ancient science of esoteric Numerology, Gnothology, each letter of the Hebrew language has a corresponding number value. The number values for the Tetragrammaton are:

YOD = 10
HE = 5
VAU = 6
HE = 5
26 = 8

Eight is twice four, and four is the important association here. The four letters of the Tetragrammaton indicate four mystical divisions, each letter having an esoteric and complex relationship with each of the other letters. Four was considered a divine number in ancient cultures, and symbolized the Deity. Many of them had four-letter names for God:

Hebrews: YHVH
Egyptians: AMON
Persians: SURA
Greeks: ΘΕΟΣ
Romans: DEUS

Many of the other occult sciences employ fourfold categorization in their disciplines. For example:

THE FOUR WORLDS OF THE CABALIST

1. The World of Emanation
2. The World of Creation
3. The World of Formation
4. The World of Action or Matter

THE FOUR ELEMENTS OF THE ALCHEMIST

1. Fire
2. Water
3. Air
4. Earth

THE FOUR QUADRANTS OF THE ASTROLOGER

1. Aries/Taurus/Gemini
2. Cancer/Leo/Virgo
3. Libra/Scorpio/Sagittarius
4. Capricorn/Aquarius/Pisces

THE FOUR SUITS OF THE TAROTOLOGIST (pronounced, "Tar-o-ól-o-gist")

1. Wands
2. Cups
3. Swords
4. Pentacles

Within the word Tarot is the Latin word ROTA, meaning "wheel." If we imagine a circular frame connected by four spokes to a central hub, with one letter of the Tetragrammaton in each quadrant, we have the Wheel of Eternal Truth, endlessly turning to create power and motion in the universe. These spokes come from the central axis of the AIN SOPH — the nucleus of God. The four letters of the word TAROT (the final T is identical to the first T, also symbolizing the Worm Ouroboros, whose tail is in his mouth, the end in the beginning) can also be seen in this wheel, and their relationship to the four letters of the Tetragrammaton — YOD HE VAU HE — can be appreciated on a spiritual, if not wholly on a conscious level, by meditation on this wheel. It can be seen on the Major Arcana card, WHEEL OF FORTUNE, and has also been reproduced on the cover of this Handbook. Another reference to keep in mind about the wheel symbol is its link to the eternal cycle of reincarnation and its implication for the soul's growth.

Another correspondence to the four letters of the Tetragrammaton is associated with the creative principle inherent in all things, from God Himself through the smallest creature:

1. YOD	= ACTIVE	= MALE	= POSITIVE
2. HE	= PASSIVE	= FEMALE	= NEGATIVE
3. VAU	= NEUTRAL	= NEUTER	= THE TRINITY = TRILITERAL NAME (YHV)
4. HE	= TRANSITION from one series to another.	=	THE TETRAGRAMMATON through the repetition of the second HE into the Divine Triad: YHV(H).

Numerology of the Tetragrammaton

The esoteric science of numbers is closely interwoven with the Tarot and the Tetragrammaton. I will attempt to go only a little way into this complex subject here, just enough to give you a feeling of how the Sacred Name is numerically involved with the cards.

The numbers 1 2 3 4 correspond with YOD HE VAU HE. The second HE, as we have seen, is a transitory character from one level or series to another. That is, the second HE merges with the YOD to become part of the ACTIVE/POSITIVE force emanating from the latter character:

YOD HE VAU HE
→ YOD HE VAU HE
→ YOD HE VAU HE etc.

YOD HE VAU (HE/YOD) HE VAU (HE/YOD) HE VAU etc.

The second HE becomes the FIRST term of the second series or level of YOD HE VAU HE, and so on. Numerically, the first three characters represent the three points of the trinity, or Divine Triad — the very representation of God himself — Father, Son and Holy Spirit.

YOD = 1
HE = 2
VAU = 3

The remaining HE, whose value is 4, is a transitional sacred force, expressing the mystical and transcendental nature of the Divine Triad (YHV), transforming and solidifying the representation of the Trinity into the Holy Name of God, YOD HE VAU HE. Numerically, we can visualize this as follows:

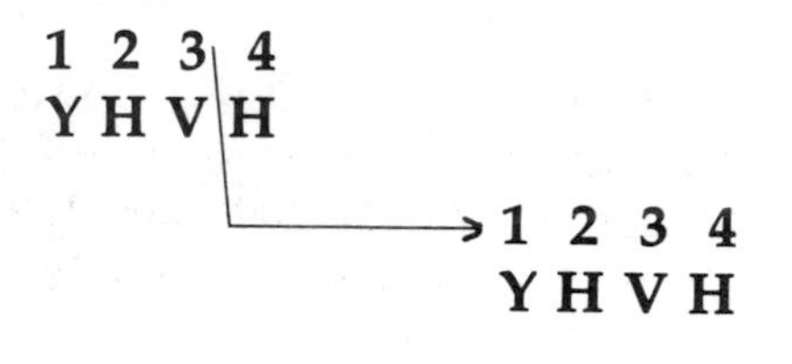

or
1 2 3 (4/1) 2 3 (4/1) 2 3 etc.

This principle is applied to the numerical value of the Minor Arcana as follows:

1 2 3 4 → **4 5 6 7** → **7 8 9 10**
Y H V H merges with **Y H V H** merges with **Y H V H** merges into the first term and now becomes the 1 of another series (10 = 1 + 0 = 1).

1 2 3 4 5 6 7 8 9 (1) 2 3 4 5 6 7 8 9 (1) 2 3 4 5 6 7 8 9 (1) 2 3 4 5 6 7 8 9 10
Y H V Y H V Y H V (Y) H V Y H V Y H V (Y) H V Y H V Y H V (Y) H V Y H V Y H V Y
WANDS CUPS SWORDS PENTACLES

From this we can derive the numerical relationship of each card in the Minor Arcana to a character of the Tetragrammaton. Thus, we can see that, for example,

ACE OF WANDS = YOD = 1
FOUR OF CUPS = YOD = 4 (second HE merges with next YOD)
SIX OF SWORDS = VAU = 6
TEN OF PENTACLES = HE = 10

The law of the Tetragrammaton also applies to the Court Cards, thus:

YOD	HE	VAU	HE
KING	QUEEN	KNIGHT	PAGE = Transition = Second HE of 10
1	2	3	
4	5	6	
7	8	9	

As for the Major Arcana, we will study their relationship to the Tetragrammaton in Chapter 6.

Although there is much more to be learned concerning the relationship between the Tetragrammaton and the Tarot, the above should be enough to give you a feeling of the subject, and to enable you to work with the Minor Mentors in a little more depth.

Comparison Chart (II)

The foregoing digression into the Tetragrammaton should make clearer the organization of the COMPARISON CHART portion of the Minor Mentors, which you will find set up as follows:

YOD
TETRAGRAMMATON
PRINCIPLE
EXPRESSION

HE
ASTROLOGY
GNOTHOLOGY

VAU
SUIT KEY
MULTIPLE
SIGNIFICANCE

HE
DIVINATION IN DEPTH:
The remaining sections of the COMPARISON CHART have to do with other occult sciences:

PRINCIPLE. This is a Cabalistic reference, also closely associated with the Tetragrammaton. The four PRINCIPLES associated with the characters of the Sacred Name are:

YOD	= SUBSTANTIALITY	= POSITIVE
HE	= IMPONDERABILITY	= NEGATIVE
VAU	= TRIALITY	= UNION
HE	= PERPETUATION	= VIBRATION

The profound significance of the Deific Name stirs the inner being and promotes power that can release man from his limited, mundane thoughts and allow the true seeker of universal wisdom access to the unlimited energies of the cosmos. If you choose to use the PRINCIPLE reference in the Mentors, you will associate each card with one of the four PRINCIPLES above:

1	2	3
YOD	HE	VAU
SUBSTANTIALITY	IMPONDERABILITY	TRIALITY

(4/5)
(HE/YOD)
(PERPETUATION/SUBSTANTIALITY) etc.

EXPRESSION. In this section, you will see groups of four key words representing all that is contained in the YOD of the Tetragrammaton: the ACTIVE FORCE of creation as considered and interpreted in many forms and languages down through the ages. Each card is symbolized by:

1. One aspect of the Holy Trinity
   1) FATHER
   2) SON
   3) HOLY SPIRIT
2. One creative aspect of the Tetragrammaton:
   1) ACTIVE
   2) PASSIVE
   3) NEUTRAL
   4) TRANSITION
3. One of the four primal elements, as utilized by Cabalists and Alchemists:
   1) FIRE
   2) WATER
   3) AIR
   4) EARTH
4. One aspect of the triune nature of God, as expressed in the Hindu pantheon:
   1) BRAHMA
   2) SIVA
   3) VISHNU

In several cases, the key word in Section 1 relates to MAN instead of God; in Section 4, it relates to NIRVANA, the state achieved by the extinction of human life and final emancipation from the cycle of reincarnation, leading to reunion with Brahma.

The next two sections of the COMPARISON CHART fall under the HE portion of the Tetragrammaton. As YOD is the positive, giving force, so HE is the negative, receiving force. The two subjects contained in the HE of the Chart are ASTROLOGY and GNOTHOLOGY, but we will only touch upon them briefly here. Like the Cabala, they are subjects of great complexity and profundity, and worthy of further study. If you already have a background of some years' study in one or both of these subjects, you will be able to bring some degree of wisdom and sensitivity to this portion of the COMPARISON CHART; but for an understanding of the Minor Mentors, it is enough to know that there is a strong connection between the Tarot and these two occult sciences.

The VAU portion of the Tetragrammaton contains three sections of the COMPARISON CHART that are of special relevance to the Tarotologist alone. They will assist you greatly in your interpretation of the Tarot symbols; by constant reference to them, you will soon become both proficient and sensitive in divination. From the force of the YOD to the receptive HE, we have the resulting factor of the union between the YOD and the HE, the VAU, which encompasses the following three sections:

1. SUIT KEY
2. MULTIPLE
3. SIGNIFICANCE

SUIT KEY. By now you should be thoroughly familiar with the SUIT KEYS, as given in Chapter 2. Little more need be said about them at this time, except to indicate that as they are now included as an important part of the Minor Mentors, you will now understand why it was important for you to master them earlier in your studies.

MULTIPLE. The MULTIPLE vibration can actually be felt by the Tarotologist as sensitivity develops. Upon completing a spread, you should observe the multiples of cards showing to determine the balance of suits. If, for example, a spread is dominated by one suit, say WANDS, the MULTIPLE reference would read: "INDICATE CHANGE." This reference would then have to be considered when interpreting the spread. Suppose that the client's question concerned his business; the overall spread would give the detail, but the reader would have to include the concept of change in his interpretation. This might be in the form of a change in business fortunes, a change of the type of business the client is engaged in, or some other type of change. This MULTIPLE influence is extremely important, and should be pursued with great diligence early in your studies.

SIGNIFICANCE. This vibration works in conjunction with the MULTIPLE reference. It is a continuation of the MULTIPLE vibration, carrying it into more specific areas of interpretation. For instance, in the above example, along with the MULTIPLE "CHANGE," you would find the SIGNIFICANCE to be "BUSINESS AND SUCCESS." This would tend to indicate a business change for the better, but the rest of the spread would have to be considered before you could say this for certain.

The final portion of the Minor Mentor COMPARISON CHART comes under the dominion of the second HE, which represents the fourth term that merges back into the active force of the YOD.

DIVINATION IN DEPTH. This is "symbology association," created by certain cards falling into particular sequences with other cards. After a spread is completed and you have assessed the "message" of the divination, you may then refer to this section for further interpretation. Like the GUIDELINES, this reference can only be properly used by a person thoroughly sensitized and experienced in divination. The examples given in the Mentors are obviously only a few of the more important associations possible, for with 78 cards plus 78 more reverse positions, the combinations are almost limitless. DIVINATION IN DEPTH is an added dimension of esoteric lore which should be considered as an extra tool for the Tarotologist.

The Court Mentors

Now that you have been introduced to the Minor Mentors, let me say just a word about the COURT MENTORS. There is not enough difference from the Minor Mentors for the COURT MENTORS to be worth a separate chapter, but it is important to remember that the Court Cards usually represent people, although they can also represent situations. The client's question, the overall spread, and the wisdom of the Tarot being sought by the reader will determine which is represented.

Now let us proceed to the more esoteric areas of the MAJOR MENTORS, and see how the references we have examined in this chapter apply to the 22 cards of the Major Arcana.

CHAPTER 6
UNDERSTANDING THE MAJOR MENTORS

When we study the Major Arcana, we find that there is an intimate relationship between the 22 cards and the Cabala or Tree of Life, as well as the Tetragrammaton, as covered in the previous chapter. The subject is too complex for me to give you more than a hint of the beauty and profundity that exists here. Those of you with a background in the Cabala will be better able to appreciate this esoteric relationship, but it is not necessary to be familiar with the Cabalistic lore to work with the Tarot successfully. I have prepared a chart on page 74 which shows the various relationships in some detail. This is merely for your contemplation and study and need not be fully understood at this point in your work with the Major Arcana.

The Tree of Life

The Cabalistic Tree of Life is a living reality in continuous movement, embracing the secrets of man in relation to the God force from which it—and he—originate. The Cabala (or Kabala) comes from the Hebrew word *Qabbalah*, meaning "doctrines received from tradition." In ancient Hebrew literature, the name denoted the entire body of theosophical and religious teachings, except for the Pentateuch. Not until the Middle Ages did the system of esoteric wisdom that we know today as Cabalism come into being, refined and studied only by Hebrew and some medieval Christian scholars.

The Tree reflects all the possibilities of man — the various choices he can and must make in his soul's journey back to God. Within its branches, man is like a bird: he can sing to the heavens and give thanks for his universal blessings as he recognizes the solidity of its trunk and senses the depths of its roots. Or he can build himself a cozy nest on one of the branches and be concerned only with his own comfort and immediate material existence, congratulating himself on his cleverness at finding security for himself and his family, and forgetting that he is actually abiding within the Tree that provides for all his needs.

The Septenaries

The Major Arcana are divided into three groups of seven cards each, called SEPTENARIES. These in turn correspond to the three main triads or TERNARIES of the Cabalistic Tree. This division intensifies in our minds the cognizance of the Divine Trinity. Each Septenary represents the progress of man on earth, and within each are the lessons man must learn to return to his heavenly heritage.

SEPTENARY ONE includes all the Major Arcana symbols represented by the active spiritual force of the YOD in the Tetragrammaton, which also embraces the influence of the second HE.

SEPTENARY TWO includes all the Major Arcana symbols represented by the passive receptive force of the first HE.

SEPTENARY THREE includes all the Major Arcana symbols represented by the resulting neutral force of the VAU.

Contained within this spiritual network lies the wisdom of the Cabala, and the intimately related Tarot deck of 78 symbols are part of its living force. The objective of any divination is to seek out the spiritual energies which correlate exactly with a given phenomenon or circumstance, much as an automobile speedometer registers and reveals the speed at which the machine is traveling.

The following chart shows how the Major Arcana are arranged into Septenaries:

CABALISTIC REFERENCE — MAJOR ARCANA

MAJOR ARCANA:		YOD and Second HE	
0 FOOL	= He = *Yod*	0 FOOL	1st Septenary = 1st Ternary
1 MAGICIAN	= Yod	4 EMPEROR	Father
2 HIGH PRIESTESS	= He	7 CHARIOT	Creator
3 EMPRESS	= Vau	10 THE WHEEL	God
4 EMPEROR	= He = *Yod*	13 DEATH	Intellectual
5 HIEROPHANT	= He	16 TOWER	Active
6 LOVERS	= Vau	19 SUN	
7 CHARIOT	= He = *Yod*		

		HE:	
8 STRENGTH	= He	2 HIGH PRIESTESS	2nd Septenary = 2nd Ternary
9 HERMIT	= Vau	5 HIEROPHANT	Son
10 THE WHEEL	= He = *Yod*	8 STRENGTH	Receiver
11 JUSTICE	= He	11 JUSTICE	Man
12 HANGED MAN	= Vau	14 TEMPERANCE	Moral
13 DEATH	= He = *Yod*	17 STAR	Passive
14 TEMPERANCE	= He	20 JUDGEMENT	

		VAU:	
15 DEVIL	= Vau	3 EMPRESS	3rd Septenary = 3rd Ternary
16 TOWER	= He = *Yod*	6 LOVERS	Spirit
17 STAR	= He	9 HERMIT	Transformer
18 MOON	= Vau	12 HANGED MAN	Universe
19 SUN	= He = *Yod*	15 DEVIL	Material
20 JUDGEMENT	= He	18 MOON	Neutral
21 WORLD	= Vau	21 WORLD	

CHART 5

THE TREE OF LIFE

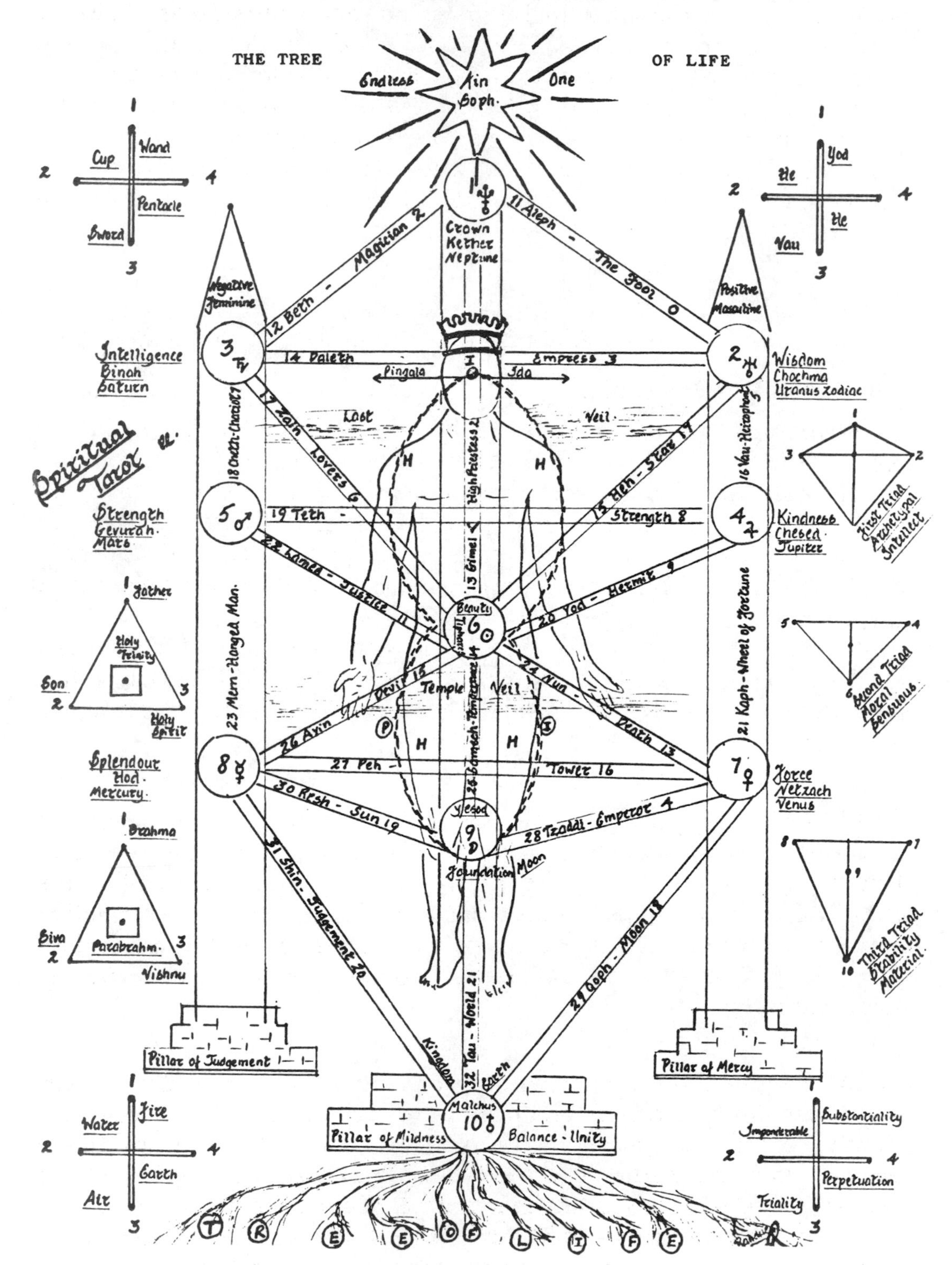
THE TREE
OF LIFE
Endless
Ain Soph
One
Wand
Cup
Pentacle
Sword
Yod
He
He
Vau
Crown
Kether
Neptune
11 Aleph - The Fool 0
12 Beth - Magician
Negative Feminine
Positive Masculine
Intelligence
Binah
Saturn
Wisdom
Chochma
Uranus Zodiac
14 Daleth
Empress 3
Pingala
Ida
Last
Veil
Spiritual Tarot
17 Zain - Lovers 6
16 Vau - Hierophant 5
15 Heh - Star 17
13 Gimel - High Priestess 2
First Triad
Archetypal
Intellect
Strength
Geburah
Mars
19 Teth
Strength 8
Kindness
Chesed
Jupiter
22 Lamed - Justice 11
20 Yod - Hermit 9
Father
Holy Trinity
Son
Holy Spirit
Beauty
Tiphareth
23 Mem - Hanged Man
21 Kaph - Wheel of Fortune
Second Triad
Moral
Sensuous
26 Ayin - Devil 15
Temple
Veil
24 Nun - Death 13
25 Samech - Temperance 14
Splendour
Hod
Mercury
27 Peh
Tower 16
Force
Netzach
Venus
30 Resh - Sun 19
Yesod
28 Tzaddi - Emperor 4
Brahma
Foundation
Moon
31 Shin - Judgement 20
29 Qoph - Moon 18
Siva
Parabrahm
Vishnu
Third Triad
Stability
Material
32 Tau - World 21
Kingdom
Earth
Pillar of Judgement
Pillar of Mercy
Malchus
Pillar of Mildness
Balance - Unity
Fire
Water
Earth
Air
Substantiality
Imponderable
Perpetuation
Triality
T R E E O F L I F E

CHART 6

Each Major Arcanum has a corresponding Major Mentor, arranged almost identically to those for the Minor Arcana and Court Cards. As in the Minor Mentors, the KEY and REVERSE KEY are intended to assist you in developing your own sensitivities and not as the only definitions of upright and reverse cards. They are to be considered as starting points only, enabling you to arrive at your own intuitive interpretations.

As in the Minor Mentors, the MEMORY is a simple two-line rhyme for each card in either position; the GUIDELINES apply here just as in the preceding chapter.

Comparison Chart

The COMPARISON CHART is set up similarly to those for the Minor and Court Mentors. In the section governed by YOD, you will find the TETRAGRAMMATON, PRINCIPLE and EXPRESSION references, as covered in the last chapter. And in the first HE section, ASTROLOGY and GNOTHOLOGY are included as before. Both of these occult sciences are closely tied to the Tarot, but there is no room to go into either in detail at this point. They are included mainly for those of you already advanced in Astrology and esoteric Numerology, so that you can understand more fully their interrelationships with the Tarot. The beginning student need not be concerned about these references.

In the section governed by VAU, however, you will find two new references replacing SUIT KEY, MULTIPLE and SIGNIFICANCE, called MEDITATION and TIME. These are of great importance to *every* student of the Tarot.

MEDITATION is a prayer especially suited to the vibration and message of each card. You should always keep in mind that although the principles of study and interpretation of the Major and Minor Arcana are similar, the former differ in depth and spiritual intensity. A deeper interpretation should be attached whenever a card is part of the Major Arcana, and an appropriate prayer should always be a part of the approach to studying any Major Arcanum.

TIME is a guide to the most appropriate time of day to meditate on each card. These time periods correlate with the varying sensitivity levels surrounding the human aura on the physical plane. It is not absolutely necessary that the meditations be conducted at the times suggested, for meditation is always rewarding at any time. But the times given will help you to be more receptive to the vibratory tones of the various Major symbols. Time has always been an important factor in religion and ritual, so whenever possible you should try to use the time elements given.

In the fourth section, governed by the second HE merging with the force of the YOD, you will find four new Cabalistic references replacing DIVINATION IN DEPTH. Unless you already have a background in Cabalistic study, you need not pay more than subliminal attention to these references. They refer to more complex relationships between the Tree of Life and the Major Arcana, and are included only for the benefit of the more advanced student.

As much as I would like to take you further into Astrology, Gnothology, and the Cabalistic correspondences of the Tarot, I do not feel it wise to do so at this stage. Perhaps these subjects can be covered at greater length in a more advanced book in the future. I have offered mere hints of the vast fields of esoteric knowledge to be found in a serious study of these occult disciplines, and the serious student who wishes to know more can seek out the information for himself. It is not necessary for you to understand the close relationship between the Tarot and the Cabala in order to work with the Tarot effectively; it is enough to know that it exists. The Tarot symbols work independently of the other occult sciences and form a complete doctrine in themselves.

Now that you have in some measure been prepared to work with the Mentors, you will find them comprising the next three chapters. Remember, don't be dismayed by the more advanced references in the Mentors. Concentrate and meditate on the ones that are familiar to you, and as your esoteric studies progress, you will find yourself drawn to and learning more about the other occult sciences. And as you study them, you will discover that they will take on added dimensions for you because of your prior knowledge of the Tarot. This in turn will lead you back to a deeper and more profound knowledge and appreciation of the Tarot itself.

CHAPTER 7
THE MINOR MENTORS

Wands

A profusion of WANDS in a spread will generally indicate a situation involving ENTERPRISE AND DISTINCTION.

WANDS SUIT KEY: ENTERPRISE AND DISTINCTION

ACE OF WANDS

KEY:
New things starting.

MEMORY:
Create, begin, invention start;
The birth, the seed's within your heart.

GUIDELINES:
Activity starting in business or social affairs.

Beginning of something new. May be job, career, or way of life.

Possible birth in the family or to someone close to you.

Look out for telephone call, letter, telegram, information. Accept any invitations offered.

REVERSE KEY:
Take stock, have a second look.

MEMORY:
Don't give up, just try again;
Plan it right and you'll know when.

GUIDELINES:
Insufficient effort, lack of initiative, simply not trying.

Other people also need consideration. Be generous in your views.

May be necessary to delay or temporarily cancel plans. No need to be depressed.

ACE OF WANDS

COMPARISON CHART:

YOD:
TETRAGRAMMATON = YOD
PRINCIPLE = Substantiality
EXPRESSION = Father/Active / Brahma/Fire

HE:
ASTROLOGY = Mercury/ Mars/Aries
GNOTHOLOGY = Individuality

VAU:
SUIT KEY = Enterprise & Distinction
MULTIPLE = Indicate Change
SIGNIFICANCE = Business & Success

HE:
DIVINATION IN DEPTH:
NEXT TO TOWER: Unable to make idea or project materialize. Frustrated and tired through effort.

PENTACLES & CUPS ON ALL SIDES: Be cheerful now, looks like good news on the way.

NEXT TO DEVIL: Analyze relationships; someone may feel hurt and is not allowing it to show.

TWO OF WANDS

KEY:
Sign of achievement in business and plans.

MEMORY:
Goals attained in work success;
Courage now brings happiness.

GUIDELINES:
Tremendous ability and foresight; future looks good.

Persevere, have courage, you can succeed.

With correct negotiation, there could be a possible business or partnership interest.

Important contract, letter or transaction indicated.

REVERSE KEY:
Foundations laid may not bring desired results.

MEMORY:
Careful planning, make no fault;
Move with caution, action halt.

GUIDELINES:
Have patience, don't spoil it now.

Need to organize and bring order to your personal life.

Don't allow anyone to dominate your thinking.

Clarify things in order to prevent any misunderstanding.

COMPARISON CHART:

YOD:
TETRAGRAMMATON = HE
PRINCIPLE = Imponderability
EXPRESSION = Son/Siva/Active/Fire

VAU:
SUIT KEY = Enterprise & Distinction.
MULTIPLE = Indicate Change
SIGNIFICANCE = Business & Success

HE:
ASTROLOGY = Virgo/Leo/Sun
GNOTHOLOGY = Cooperation

HE:
DIVINATION IN DEPTH:
NEXT TO EMPRESS OR EMPEROR: Opportunity imminent; establish yourself and set ideas into motion.

SWORDS ON ALL SIDES: A "time element," new vibrations coming in; get everything in order.

NEXT TO SEVEN OF SWORDS: Unnecessary disturbance over insignificant situation; sort out any problems.

THREE OF WANDS

KEY:
Someone willing to give assistance; partnership or cooperation possible.

MEMORY:
Help is offered to those in need;
Cooperation will plant the seed.

GUIDELINES:
Right teammate could enhance a project and bring required success.

Someone knowledgeable can give you the help you need.

Seeds planted for business venture can prosper.

REVERSE KEY:
Talents, skills, efforts being wasted; new direction needed.

MEMORY:
Utilize your skills and know
Castles from foundations grow.

GUIDELINES:
A careless approach could spoil everything.

Check all information before moving ahead with new ventures.

Being proud or overly confident is the wrong attitude to take, could mean a downfall.

COMPARISON CHART:

YOD:
TETRAGRAMMATON = VAU
PRINCIPLE = Triality
EXPRESSION = Holy Spirit/Vishnu/Active/Fire

VAU:
SUIT KEY = Enterprise & Distinction
MULTIPLE = Indicate Change
SIGNIFICANCE = Business & Success

HE:
ASTROLOGY = Libra/Aries/Sagittarius/Mars/Jupiter
GNOTHOLOGY = Self-expression

HE:

DIVINATION IN DEPTH:
STRENGTH OR JUSTICE IN SPREAD: Eventually you will benefit from all your efforts. Keep going, you will receive your reward.

NEXT TO HIGH PRIESTESS: Spiritual goals will give you a deeper understanding and awaken your intuitive powers.

NEXT TO WHEEL OF FORTUNE: A positive attitude will win the day.

FOUR OF WANDS

KEY:
Harmony, peace and satisfaction.

MEMORY:
Harmony, peace now has grown;
The finest harvest you'll bring home.

GUIDELINES:
Job well done. Satisfaction and peace now coming your way.

Now is the time to plan and enjoy the results of hard work.

Someone enjoying romance could be laying foundations for marriage.

REVERSE KEY:
Positive improvement; well on the way to achievement.

MEMORY:
Look around, your blessings see:
Be thankful, lest they fly from thee.

GUIDELINES:
If you care, show it. You may lose someone or something because of your attitude.

Take your mind off the so-called big things and learn to appreciate things that really matter.

Be thankful for what you have.

COMPARISON CHART:

YOD:
TETRAGRAMMATON = YOD
PRINCIPLE = Substantiality
EXPRESSION = Father/Brahma/Active/Fire

VAU:
SUIT KEY = Enterprise & Distinction
MULTIPLE = Indicate Change
SIGNIFICANCE = Business & Success

HE:
ASTROLOGY = Leo/Sun/Scorpio
GNOTHOLOGY = Self-discipline

HE:

DIVINATION IN DEPTH:
NEXT TO HERMIT: Extremely individual person with the ability of self-expression; creative when alone.

NEXT TO MAGICIAN: Exciting originality, ideas, projects and goals.

NEXT TO WORLD: Powerful vibrations; possible opportunity to be involved in large-scale operations.

FIVE OF WANDS

KEY:
Opposing energies create agitation.

MEMORY:
Struggle, endeavor, labor and strife;
Competing strongly, sharp as a knife.

GUIDELINES:
You are feeling the stress of continuous competition.

Situation now calls for clarity; be firm and state the facts.

Don't be afraid to give the facts to get the cooperation you require.

REVERSE KEY:
Harmony and a sense of peace will prevail.

MEMORY:
New vibrations of peace and love;
Feel well blessed from Heaven above.

GUIDELINES:
Watch out for exciting new opportunities. Keep body and mind in trim.

Be prepared to accept a flow of harmonious vibrations into your life.

Don't be defensive; enjoy generosity and attention from others.

COMPARISON CHART:

YOD:
TETRAGRAMMATON = HE
PRINCIPLE = Imponderability
EXPRESSION = Son/Siva/Active/Fire

VAU:
SUIT KEY = Enterprise & Distinction
MULTIPLE = Indicate Change
SIGNIFICANCE = Business & Success

HE:
ASTROLOGY = Jupiter/Leo/Sagittarius/Sun

GNOTHOLOGY = Freedom

HE:
DIVINATION IN DEPTH:
NEXT TO HERMIT: Don't rely on anyone; whatever needs accomplishing can only be achieved by you.

SUN AND STAR TO LEFT AND RIGHT OR ABOVE AND BELOW THE FIVE OF WANDS: Don't be concerned about others. This Karmic lesson will give you deeper understanding with prosperity.

NEXT TO DEVIL: Don't waste energies trying to make amends; no one is interested at this time.

SIX OF WANDS

KEY:
Have faith; you can win.

MEMORY:
Good news coming, success near,
Winning all that you hold dear.

GUIDELINES:
You are going to succeed; keep trying.

Relationships will get better; possible journey as a leader or representative.

Efforts directed toward the arts or sciences will prove successful.

REVERSE KEY:
Unable to get it together; things don't appear to gel.

MEMORY:
Whichever way you try to go,
Try as you may won't make it so.

GUIDELINES:
Recognition or payment due delayed at this time.

Be careful that your sense of pride does not hurt your reputation.

Don't build up tension or pressure, even though you think someone may be trying to take advantage of you.

COMPARISON CHART:

YOD:
TETRAGRAMMATON = VAU
PRINCIPLE = Triality
EXPRESSION = Holy Spirit/Vishnu/Active/Fire

HE:
ASTROLOGY = Venus/Leo/Aries/Sun/Mars
GNOTHOLOGY = Harmony

VAU:
SUIT KEY = Enterprise & Distinction.
MULTIPLE = Indicate Change
SIGNIFICANCE = Business & Success

HE:
DIVINATION IN DEPTH:
NEXT TO FOOL: There are still obstacles ahead. Don't be lax.

NEXT TO HIGH PRIESTESS: Because of the present vibratory cycle, you will be inclined to seek out more knowledge of metaphysical philosophy.

NEXT TO HIEROPHANT: Strong indication of a person who understands the needs of others; has a good position, well established, could be generous to you.

SEVEN OF WANDS

KEY:

You are well blessed with inner strength.

MEMORY:
A soul with courage can win through;
Problems now are not for you.

GUIDELINES:
Strong character; can hold on in any adversity.

Under pressure at work or in some other situation.

Rest from undue tensions; you will see things more clearly.

REVERSE KEY:
Plumb your own depths and feel the strength within.

MEMORY:
This is not the time to fear;
All will pass, peace is near.

GUIDELINES:
Your position is stronger than you think. Don't let anyone take advantage of you.

Don't be indecisive; he who hesitates is lost.

Have patience; don't make unwise decisions or feel threatened.

COMPARISON CHART:
YOD:
TETRAGRAMMATON = YOD
PRINCIPLE = Substantiality
EXPRESSION = Father/Brahma/Active/Fire

VAU:
SUIT KEY = Enterprise & Distinction
MULTIPLE = Indicate Change
SIGNIFICANCE = Business & Success

HE:
ASTROLOGY = Sagittarius/Jupiter
GNOTHOLOGY = Wisdom —Inner Self

HE:
DIVINATION IN DEPTH:
NEXT TO HANGED MAN: Being stubborn will not solve anything. Don't be afraid to submit; it will not reflect on your character.

NEXT TO DEATH: Perhaps you are going about things the wrong way; slow down — it isn't worth it.

NEXT TO TEMPERANCE: More time is needed to achieve your goal; why not think things over a little?

EIGHT OF WANDS

KEY:
Acceleration in your affairs; movement, news coming in.

MEMORY:
Movement, progress, action, speed;
Trip or message that you need.

GUIDELINES:
Goal within reach; new ideas will bring satisfactory conclusions.

To have control, the budget must balance.

Indication of travel in connection with business.

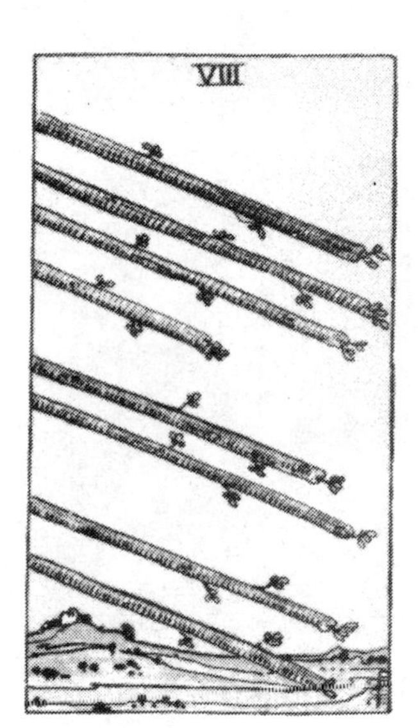

REVERSE KEY:
Apprehension creates an insecure feeling.

MEMORY:
Insecurity brings the storm;
Some fears end, some are born.

GUIDELINES:
Control emotions; quarrels or jealousy will not solve problems.

Easy now, force or pressure could ruin all your plans.

It might help if you thought about it more; a slight adjustment could change everything.

COMPARISON CHART:

YOD:
TETRAGRAMMATON = HE
PRINCIPLE = Imponderability
EXPRESSION = Son/Siva/Active/Fire

HE:
ASTROLOGY = Sagittarius/Aries/Capricorn/Jupiter/Mars
GNOTHOLOGY = Executive Power & Ability

VAU:
SUIT KEY = Enterprise & Distinction
MULTIPLE = Indicate Change
SIGNIFICANCE = Business & Success

HE:
DIVINATION IN DEPTH:
NEXT TO SUN: Charm is the keynote here. Anticipate a pleasant gathering, good vibrations.

NEXT TO LOVERS: Warm, genuine conversations taking place, promises being given, future being discussed.

NEXT TO DEVIL: Ignore temptation to forge ahead; reconsider everything and the conseqences.

NINE OF WANDS

KEY:
You are able to maintain control of your interests. Must use discretion in any forthcoming venture.

MEMORY:
So far, so good, go on this way;
Take time to hear what others say.

GUIDELINES:
Protect your own affairs but don't show obstinacy.

Hold on to what you believe; you have the strength to see it through.

You have the knowledge and the ability to persevere.

REVERSE KEY:
Not applying yourself; you lack initiative.

MEMORY:
Be prepared to take command;
Inferior plans just will not stand.

GUIDELINES:
You are not properly prepared; this can make you vulnerable.

Try not to bend under adversity; tendency to display weakness in attitude.

Fight for what you believe to be right and true.

COMPARISON CHART:

YOD:
TETRAGRAMMATON = VAU
PRINCIPLE = Triality
EXPRESSION = Holy Spirit/Vishnu/Active/Fire

VAU:
SUIT KEY = Enterprise & Distinction
MULTIPLE = Indicate Change
SIGNIFICANCE = Business & Success

HE:
ASTROLOGY = Leo/Jupiter/Sun/Aquarius/Sagittarius
GNOTHOLOGY = Universalism

HE:
DIVINATION IN DEPTH:
NEXT TO SUN: Denotes personal or business interests pertaining to vacation areas and/or properties.

NEXT TO TEN OF WANDS: Negotiations regarding real estate, building, rental, purchasing, etc.

NEXT TO MAGICIAN: May refer to business enquiry regarding books and/or metaphysical supplies and interests.

TEN OF WANDS

KEY:
You have been under pressure and experienced many changes in life.

MEMORY:
Vibrations changing all around;
Seeds are deep within the ground.

GUIDELINES:
Indicates an oppressive burden, physically and mentally.

It's the darkness before the dawn.

Tremendous responsibilities; perhaps you prefer life this way.

REVERSE KEY:
Talent, ability, skills, etc., used in the wrong way.

MEMORY:
Gifts abused can bring grief;
Now's the time to turn the leaf.

GUIDELINES:
Indication of a clever person trying to unload his burden on others.

Out of sequence; energies going in the wrong direction.

Need to take another look at original goal to see if still on course.

TEN OF WANDS

COMPARISON CHART:

YOD:
TETRAGRAMMATON = HE
PRINCIPLE = Perpetuation
EXPRESSION = Nirvana/Man/Active/Fire

HE:
ASTROLOGY = Uranus/Leo/Sun
GNOTHOLOGY = Individuality

VAU:
SUIT KEY = Enterprise & Distinction
MULTIPLE = Indicate Change
SIGNIFICANCE = Business & Success

HE:
DIVINATION IN DEPTH:
NEXT TO FOOL: Look carefully into the sequence of cards following the Fool; they should help show where you have miscalculated or misjudged a situation that needs reconsideration or correction.

PENTACLES & CUPS ON ALL SIDES: Growth of the right kind; indicates prosperity for business or other enterprise.

NEXT TO STAR: It will happen soon! Ventures undertaken will be successful.

Cups

A profusion of CUPS in a spread will generally indicate a situation involving LOVE AND HAPPINESS.

CUPS SUIT KEY: LOVE AND HAPPINESS

ACE OF CUPS

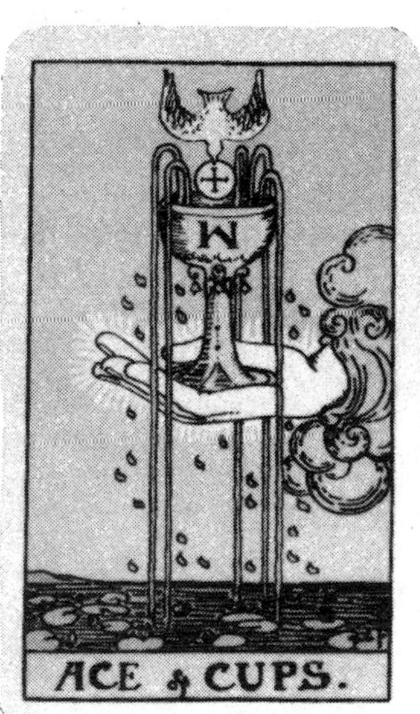

KEY:
Beginning of all good things: love, joy, health.

MEMORY:
Joy within the home and heart;
Blessings come with this new start.

GUIDELINES:
New spiritual insight and sensitivity developing.

Activities regarding present home or a new home.

Changes in affairs that affect the home which will result in happiness for all concerned.

Making a new start; attend to small details and everything will work out fine.

The start of a love affair.

REVERSE KEY:
Egotistical and self-centered.

MEMORY:
Let your ego now deflate;
See how others then relate.

GUIDELINES:
Disgruntled, bored, in a rut. Need for a change.

New goals needed; lack of energy due to non-activity.

Spiritual refreshment will give deeper insight. Allow the Inner Self to explore and find purpose.

Need for balance; you love too intensely or not enough.

Depression, feeling unwanted.

ACE OF CUPS

COMPARISON CHART:

YOD:
TETRAGRAMMATON = YOD
PRINCIPLE = Substantiality
EXPRESSION = Father/Brahma /Passive/Water

HE:
ASTROLOGY = Mercury/ Cancer/Moon
GNOTHOLOGY = Individuality

VAU:
SUIT KEY = Love & Happiness
MULTIPLE = Love & Emotions
SIGNIFICANCE = Joy & Affection

HE:

DIVINATION IN DEPTH:

SWORDS ON ALL SIDES: Conditions in the home are not settled; circumstances affecting this situation should be revealed in the spread.

NEXT TO WHEEL OF FORTUNE: Financial affairs should now be greatly improved; indication of additional money or income.

NEXT TO LOVERS: A definite improvement in family relationships; family matters are no longer troubled.

TWO OF CUPS

KEY:
Understanding, deep friendship or love between man and woman. Together they can achieve their plans.

MEMORY:
Harmony flows between two souls;
Together they will reach their goals.

GUIDELINES:
A beautiful start to a new romance or friendship.

A complimentary seed has flowered into a tree of appreciation.

Good solid ideas passing back and forth between two people.

Kindness and thoughtfulness binds two hearts together.

Expect a surprise: letter, gift, flowers or joyous event.

REVERSE KEY:
Unimportant disagreement has raised obstacles. It can be solved but someone must make the first move.

MEMORY:
Misunderstanding dims the day;
Get together, there's a way.

GUIDELINES:
Loss of balance in a close relationship; it doesn't matter who makes the first move.

You should not be possessive or too demanding in a relationship.

Pride destroys love. The artificial protection of your ego is not worth it.

It's not always possible to have everything perfect; all-or-nothing-at-all attitude will deprive you of what you need.

Getting upset will not help matters; try to think things over and get a new perspective.

TWO OF CUPS

COMPARISON CHART:

YOD:
TETRAGRAMMATON = HE
PRINCIPLE = Imponderability
EXPRESSION = Son/Siva/Passive/Water

VAU:
SUIT KEY = Love & Happiness
MULTIPLE = Love & Emotions
SIGNIFICANCE = Joy & Affection

HE:
ASTROLOGY = Virgo/Cancer/Scorpio/Moon/Pluto/Mars
GNOTHOLOGY = Cooperation

HE:
DIVINATION IN DEPTH:
NEXT TO TOWER: Readjustment of a personal relationship due to new circumstances. Could be unexpected news causing stress or pressure.

NEXT TO HIGH PRIESTESS: You may feel insecure regarding a loved one. Unable to penetrate partner's depth, you feel incomplete.

NEXT TO SUN: Great love and understanding shared, two people will enjoy many blessings.

THREE OF CUPS

KEY:
Happy conclusion, success and the beginning of a new lifestyle is yours.

MEMORY:
Abundance, joy, hopes
complete;
Fulfillment can be very
sweet.

GUIDELINES:
Anticipation; something good is on the way.

Could indicate pregnancy.

Hospitality in the air, parties, celebration or bridal shower.

Indication of metaphysical interests; talent and sensitivity lie hidden just beneath the surface.

REVERSE KEY:
Circumstances have changed; what was good is now causing pain. Don't dwell on this, but turn right around and concentrate your energies in a different direction.

MEMORY:
What was good now
brings pain;
Remember sunshine follows rain.

GUIDELINES:
Overindulgence creating problems; time to straighten up and take charge again.

Don't let idle conversation from an old friend bother you.

Time to take command of yourself; make new plans and look ahead.

Fill your life with new interests; don't feel sorry for yourself, you have much to accomplish.

THREE OF CUPS

COMPARISON CHART:

YOD:

TETRAGRAMMATON = VAU
PRINCIPLE: = Triality
EXPRESSION = Holy Spirit/ Vishnu/Passive/ Water

HE:

ASTROLOGY = Libra/Cancer/ Pisces/Moon/ Neptune/Jupiter
GNOTHOLOGY = Self-expression

VAU:

SUIT KEY = Love & Happiness
MULTIPLE = Love & Emotions
SIGNIFICANCE = Joy & Affection

HE: DIVINATION IN DEPTH:

NEXT TO HIEROPHANT: Unusual or unconventional type of gathering: specialized meeting/ convention to which everyone concerned is looking forward.

NEXT TO DEATH: Complete change in lifestyle or work. New places, new faces, like starting all over again.

NEXT TO TEMPERANCE: Moderation; take your time to get accustomed to exciting changes. Adapt gradually to new experiences.

FOUR OF CUPS

KEY:
Discontent, boredom; need for re-evaluation.

MEMORY:
Discontent, feel quite
alone;
Experience has no profits shown.

GUIDELINES:
Couldn't care less what really happens. No motivation.

Too much of a good thing, life too easy, just won't make the effort.

Emotionally introverted, looking for a spiritual level of satisfaction. No one seems to understand.

Could be a party in the offing that will help brighten things up.

REVERSE KEY:
New relationship now possible.

MEMORY:
Results now are coming
through:
People now are hearing
you.

GUIDELINES:
Great desire to accomplish something; achievement seems far away.

There will be a positive change; stop worrying.

Rome was not built in a day! Ideas are good but need working on; have more patience.

May appear that nothing is happening, but be prepared for an exciting turn of events.

FOUR OF CUPS

COMPARISON CHART:

YOD:
TETRAGRAMMATON = YOD
PRINCIPLE = Substantiality
EXPRESSION = Father/Brahma/ Passive/Water

HE:
ASTROLOGY = Scorpio/Pluto/ Mars
GNOTHOLOGY = Self-discipline

VAU:
SUIT = Love & Happiness
MULTIPLE = Love & Emotions
SIGNIFICANCE = Joy & Affection

HE:
DIVINATION IN DEPTH:
NEXT TO WHEEL OF FORTUNE: A new interest within the next 14-day cycle. You should become involved; it will eliminate your present dilemma.

NEXT TO HANGED MAN: Feeling sorry for yourself. Nobody likes the company of someone who is miserable. Shake out of it, make some phone calls and contacts.

NEXT TO HERMIT: A gentle peace and satisfaction surround you; you are enjoying this solitude and experiencing spiritual refreshment.

FIVE OF CUPS

KEY:
You find it difficult to explain the turmoil you feel inside.

MEMORY:
Deep sorrow takes a
while to heal;
Pleasures of life do not
seem real.

GUIDELINES:
Marriage or relationship appears to be breaking up.

At this midway point, take stock of things before making another major decision.

Check spread very carefully; could indicate loss of a loved one.

The damage has been done; no use crying over split milk.

REVERSE KEY:
Things are now looking better; you have the courage to see things through.

MEMORY:
Courage will blossom
from broken
dreams;
Life is not what it seems.

GUIDELINES:
There is hope; it is not the end but an opportunity for a new beginning.

Could be happy news! A get-together with an old friend or loved one.

It would be good to consider a new home or working environment.

Don't be afraid to start building new ideas and plans; you have learned well from past experience.

FIVE OF CUPS

COMPARISON CHART:

YOD:
TETRAGRAMMATON = HE
PRINCIPLE = Imponderability
EXPRESSION = Son/Siva/Passive/Water

HE:
ASTROLOGY = Jupiter/Scorpio/Pisces/Pluto/Mars/Neptune
GNOTHOLOGY = Freedom

VAU:
SUIT KEY = Love & Happiness
MULTIPLE = Love & Emotions
SIGNIFICANCE = Joy & Affection

HE:
DIVINATION IN DEPTH:
A MINIMUM OF THREE WAND CARDS PLUS WHEEL OF FORTUNE IN THE SPREAD: Time for action! Career or negotiations are now possible. Vital that you act immediately and leave behind your sorrows.

JUDGEMENT OR STAR IN SPREAD: Karmic conditions has passed; with spiritual debt paid there is now a blessing for new endeavors.

NEXT TO DEVIL: Indication that time must be spent in contemplation. Too many wasted energies; get back on the track.

SIX OF CUPS

KEY:
From the past will come happiness. Possible to meet an old friend or acquaintance.

MEMORY:
Happiness comes from
days gone by;
Child-like joy stirs old
tie.

GUIDELINES:
Could meet an old friend who has a gift or special news for you.

You may be presented with a chance to relocate or a new job offer.

Possible to make a new friend who will have much in common.

There could be an inheritance which will bring surprises.

REVERSE KEY:
Rewards may be delayed or someone may receive recognition that you feel is due you.

MEMORY:
Delays will test your
strength and will;
Don't react, be quite still.

GUIDELINES:
A trip or some special event you've been looking forward to may be postponed.

Come out of the past and live in today. Times are changing.

Disappointed with something received; could be an inheritance.

Need to get out of a relationship or a stifling situation.

SIX OF CUPS

COMPARISON CHART:

YOD:
TETRAGRAMMATON = VAU
PRINCIPLE = Triality
EXPRESSION = Holy Spirit/ Vishnu/Passive/ Water

HE:
ASTROLOGY = Venus/Scorpio/Cancer/ Pluto/Mars/ Moon
GNOTHOLOGY = Harmony

VAU:
SUIT KEY = Love & Happiness
MULTIPLE = Love & Emotions
SIGNIFICANCE = Joy & Affection

HE:
DIVINATION IN DEPTH: NEXT TO MOON: Some concern from the past was never really understood; need to clean out the closet and allow yourself to see the situation realistically.

NEXT TO STRENGTH: You have the ability to achieve your goals; old dreams can become new, shining, attainable ideas.

NEXT TO HIEROPHANT, EMPEROR OR EMPRESS: Meaningful relationships are clouded with misunderstanding or lack of tolerance. This Karmic lesson must be understood and corrected.

SEVEN OF CUPS

KEY:
You are experiencing difficulties in making a decision.

MEMORY:
When choices are many,
and you can't see
Woods for trees, then let
it be.

GUIDELINES:
Be realistic: narrow down your choices with plain common sense.

Wake up and do what you must do.

Unexpected event will take place; it will be beneficial and improve your attitude.

A definite change for the better; life works in cycles.

REVERSE KEY:
On the right track; you should pursue your goal.

MEMORY:
Follow your goal and
don't waste time;
Success is yours down
the line.

GUIDELINES:
Watch for any glimmer of success and follow it through.

Don't give up your ideas; it may be hard to carry them through but ignore any opposition.

Offer your insecurity up in prayer and it will be replaced with spiritual strength.

Persist in studying and you can reap great rewards.

SEVEN OF CUPS

COMPARISON CHART:

YOD:
TETRAGRAMMATON = YOD
PRINCIPLE = Substantiality
EXPRESSION = Father/Brahma/ Passive/Water

HE:
ASTROLOGY = Sagittarius/ Pisces/Neptune/Jupiter
GNOTHOLOGY = Wisdom —Inner Self

VAU:
SUIT KEY = Love & Happiness
MULTIPLE = Love & Emotions
SIGNIFICANCE = Joy & Affection

HE:
DIVINATION IN DEPTH:

NEXT TO WORLD: Rid yourself of all fears. Take a good look at your life. Be prepared to make decisions, and attainment can be yours.

NEXT TO LOVERS: Your life path is broad enough for two. Be considerate of someone close when making important changes in your life.

NEXT TO WHEEL OF FORTUNE: Seek out the right advice before moving ahead. With the correct guidance you can become very successful.

EIGHT OF CUPS

KEY:
A need to search for deeper meaning in life.

MEMORY:
The Higher Self must
now proceed
To search and find the
Inner need.

GUIDELINES:
You have a need for spiritual fulfillment, are tired of your old ways.

It has become necessary to look for other alternatives.

You're totally dissatisfied and disappointed with progress to date.

You want to do something entirely different, but you don't know what.

REVERSE KEY:
Interests lie in material pleasures.

MEMORY:
Pursuing pleasure, having fun;
Not much thought for
anyone.

GUIDELINES:
Can mean a new love interest is on the way.

An urgent need for money; you're willing to work for it.

You desire a complete change; you're bored with present life style.

Not the right time to settle down. Must be absolutely sure before making any changes.

EIGHT OF CUPS

COMPARISON CHART:

YOD:
TETRAGRAMMATON = HE
PRINCIPLE = Imponderability
EXPRESSION = Son/Siva/ Passive/Water

HE:
ASTROLOGY = Capricorn/ Pisces/Cancer/ Neptune/Jupiter
GNOTHOLOGY = Executive Power & Ability

VAU:
SUIT KEY = Love & happiness
MULTIPLE = Love & Emotions
SIGNIFICANCE = Joy & Affection

HE:
DIVINATION IN DEPTH:

NEXT TO MAGICIAN: You have within your grasp the ability to reach the top. Think carefully before making a choice. Do what you know is right and don't be put off by outside opinions.

NEXT TO HERMIT: Realization and inner joy will be your reward. Be patient and forge ahead.

NEXT TO CHARIOT: Contain yourself more and channel your energies toward achieving your goal. Don't get involved in unnecessary situations or gossip.

NINE OF CUPS

KEY:
Known as the "Wish Card." Spread position is important. Can mean "wish come true," especially in the tenth Celtic Position.* Other cards will determine how.

MEMORY:
Nine of Cups, wish come true;
What you want will come to you.

GUIDELINES:
Much happiness, future assured, material gains.

Good health and a sense of well-being.

Reaching for the heights seems easier now.

Worries are disappearing and new plans are materializing.

REVERSE KEY:
Wish will not be fulfilled at this time.

MEMORY:
Look and find some other way;
Your wish will come another day.

GUIDELINES:
Insufficient funds for project or personal needs.

Check diet! Maybe too much food or drink.

A feeling of being deprived; limited view of success.

Can suggest minor illness; you should take better care of your health.

*See Chapter 11.

NINE OF CUPS

COMPARISON CHART:

YOD:
TETRAGRAMMATON = VAU
PRINCIPLE = Triality
EXPRESSION = Holy spirit/ Vishnu/Passive/ Water

VAU:
SUIT KEY = Love & Happiness
MULTIPLE = Love & Emotions
SIGNIFICANCE = Joy & Affection

HE:
ASTROLOGY = Aquarius/ Pisces/Scorpio/ Neptune/Jupiter/ Pluto/Mars
GNOTHOLOGY = Universal-ism

HE:
DIVINATION IN DEPTH: The positive vibrations of this symbol are affected by all Major Arcana symbols that appear nearby in the spread and should be interpreted accordingly. Although the Nine of Cups denotes a positive YES to your query, the way in which it will be answered can be found in the Major Arcana cards surrounding the Nine of Cups.

TEN OF CUPS

KEY:
You are experiencing the state of happiness you desire. Realization of personal hopes and dreams.

MEMORY:
Peace within, content-
ment reigns;
Joy at last after pains.

GUIDELINES:
Indication of marriage; look into the spread for confirmation.

Difficult for you to realize that everything is working out well.

Possible trip that spells happiness.

Things happening suddenly! Exciting vibrations.

REVERSE KEY:
Present situation surrounding you is causing depression or sadness.

MEMORY:
Time heals the aching
heart;
Soon the sadness will
depart.

GUIDELINES:
Futile disagreements; perhaps a family upset.

A terrible feeling of being let down.

Feelings hurt; thoughtless actions have caused tears.

Could indicate loss of a friend or someone dear.

TEN OF CUPS

COMPARISON CHART:

YOD:

TETRAGRAMMATON = HE
PRINCIPLE = Perpetuation
EXPRESSION = Nirvana/Man/Passive/Water

HE:

ASTROLOGY = Uranus/Scorpio/Pluto/Mars
GNOTHOLOGY = Individuality

VAU:

SUIT KEY = Love & Happiness
MULTIPLE = Love & Emotions
SIGNIFICANCE = Joy & Affection

HE:

DIVINATION IN DEPTH:

NEXT TO ANY TENS: A change is imminent. The number of tens in the spread indicates how radical the change will be.

NEXT TO TOWER: A very definite change in life. Look to the spread for further details.

NEXT TO EMPRESS: A good time to make plans for the future with someone close.

Swords

A profusion of SWORDS in a spread will generally indicate a situation involving STRUGGLE AND ANIMOSITY.

SWORDS SUIT KEY: STRUGGLE AND ANIMOSITY

ACE OF SWORDS

KEY:
The seeds of success and triumph are now taking root.

MEMORY:
Success takes root, triumph is near;
Soon your worries will disappear.

GUIDELINES:
Worried, depressed, sad. Anxiously expecting the worst to happen.

If you want change, you can make it happen.

Make long-term goals and plan ahead; keep your thoughts on the happiness of tomorrow.

It is not the end of everything, it is the beginning of something new; forget the past and put your energies into new ideas and plans.

REVERSE KEY:
Careful, don't apply any more pressure to achieve your goals at this time.

MEMORY:
Gently does it, do not push;
You could lose all in a rush.

GUIDELINES:
Look for any weak spots in your plans; make sure all is in order.

You may receive opposition, and this could cause delay.

Check everything before going ahead; you will save time by doing this.

Obstacles may arise; don't be hasty, but prepare by planning efficiently.

ACE OF SWORDS

COMPARISION CHART:

YOD:

TETRAGRAMMATON = YOD
PRINCIPLE = Substantiality
EXPRESSION = Father/Brahma/ Neutral/Earth

VAU:

SUIT KEY = Struggle & Animosity
MULTIPLE = Struggle & Effort
SIGNIFICANCE = Continual Effort & Endeavor

HE:

ASTROLOGY = Mercury/Capricorn/Saturn
GNOTHOLOGY = Individuality

HE:

DIVINATION IN DEPTH:

NEXT TO WORLD: Sign of obstinate attitude, reluctant to accept advice, consider any help offered as interference.

NEXT TO HIEROPHANT: You have tried many ways to improve your life, career, etc. Energies need consolidation. Must direct yourself toward one specific goal, not divide concentration.

NEXT TO WHEEL OF FORTUNE: Feeling of hopelessness, no way out. Each way you turn seems a dead end. Need to start again and not be distracted by other possibilities.

TWO OF SWORDS

KEY:
You don't know what to do; choice is six of one, half a dozen of another.

MEMORY:
Shall I do this? Shall I do that?
Need to find a new format.

GUIDELINES:
Stalemate in your affairs; need for a new approach.

Emotions are involved; difficult to decide what to do.

Recognition, success in some venture. Not sure which way to go next.

Indication of being upset by a letter or situation.

REVERSE KEY:
Things are happening now; you're able to make decisions; care is needed.

MEMORY:
Free to make your own decision;
Do it now with fine precision.

GUIDELINES:
Affairs may be moving very quickly; don't let the pace get you down.

If possible, give yourself time to think before committing yourself to anything.

Be sure that you are dealing with the right person; until you are, don't share any confidences.

Put off making any decisions until you are absolutely sure.

TWO OF SWORDS

COMPARISON CHART:

YOD:
TETRAGRAMMATON = HE
PRINCIPLE = Imponderability
EXPRESSION = Son/Siva/Neutral/Earth

HE:
ASTROLOGY = Virgo/Capricorn/Taurus/Saturn/Venus
GNOTHOLOGY = Cooperation

VAU:
SUIT KEY = Struggle & Animosity
MULTIPLE = Struggle & Effort
SIGNIFICANCE = Continual Effort & Endeavor

HE:
DIVINATION IN DEPTH:
NEXT TO MOON: Worry can affect your health. Don't allow your imagination to inflate your concerns. Get a grip on yourself and think positively.

NEXT TO SUN: Hold on to your beliefs, all is not lost; you'll be back in the world of action very soon.

SWORDS ON ALL SIDES: Always the darkest before the dawn! Don't cut yourself off from loved ones. Let them help, they will understand.

THREE OF SWORDS

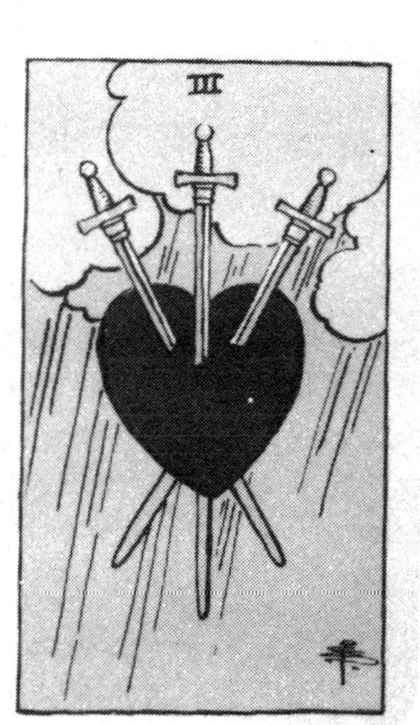

KEY:
It is hard to bear the pain of separation or to understand why we can be inflicted with such deep sorrow.

MEMORY:
Upheaval causes deep distress;
Separation or loneliness.

GUIDELINES:
Quarreling can cause a separation; try to solve the problem.

Upheaval in family situation, upset and tears.

Could indicate a miscarriage or abortion.

Due to misfortune, loved ones are separated, causing misery to those concerned.

REVERSE KEY:
Similar interpretation, but the situation or circumstances are not so severe.

MEMORY:
Upset, tears, all has gone;
Aching heart needs someone.

GUIDELINES:
Too much disorder and confusion; need for organization.

Petty quarrels can lead to serious disagreements.

Be the peacemaker; although it may be difficult, someone has to say he is sorry.

Think before you speak; don't feel sorry after it's too late.

THREE OF SWORDS

COMPARISON CHART:

YOD:
TETRAGRAMMATON = VAU
PRINCIPLE = Triality
EXPRESSION = Holy Spirit/Vishnu/Neutral/Earth

HE:
ASTROLOGY = Libra/Capricorn/Virgo/Saturn/Mercury
GNOTHOLOGY = Self-expression

VAU:
SUIT KEY = Struggle & Animosity
MULTIPLE = Struggle & Effort
SIGNIFICANCE = Continual Effort & Endeavor

HE:
DIVINATION IN DEPTH:
LOVERS IN THE SPREAD PLUS SWORDS ON ALL SIDES: This combination indicates the severing of a close relationshiop.

NEXT TO EMPEROR: Hurt by the harshness of criticism or unfair judgement. Do not pursue or try to change things. Start fresh and don't be afraid.

NEXT TO WORLD: A Karmic situation is nearly over. Prepare for new events in your life; the future holds much promise.

FOUR OF SWORDS

KEY:
Feeling of being cut off and out of touch. Take this time to think of new plans for the future.

MEMORY:
Time to think and contemplate;
Dreams come true but you must wait.

GUIDELINES:
Be prepared, things are changing; make your plans now.

Give yourself time; situation getting better, no hurry.

Indicates a convalescent period: time to renew energies both physical and mental.

The shadow over your life is slowly moving away.

REVERSE KEY:
Back into action again! Good opportunities ahead, but tread carefully.

MEMORY:
Need for action, move with care;
Of indiscretion be aware.

GUIDELINES:
Use discretion, be careful, think before you commit yourself.

Feeling of opposition; difficult to get things moving.

Indication of unrest and problems at place of work.

Don't make promises at this time; situation could rapidly change.

FOUR OF SWORDS

COMPARISON CHART:
YOD:
TETRAGRAMMATON = YOD
PRINCIPLE = Substantiality
EXPRESSION = Father/Brahma/ Neutral/Earth

VAU:
SUIT KEY = Struggle & Animosity
MULTIPLE = Struggle & Effort
SIGNIFICANCE = Continual Effort & Endeavor

HE:
ASTROLOGY = Scorpio/Taurus/ Venus
GNOTHOLOGY = Self-discipline

HE:
DIVINATION IN DEPTH:
NEXT TO ANY ACE: Need to re-evaluate any long-term plans or other considerations. Although you may not yet be involved, check everything before going ahead.

THREE OR MORE COURT CARDS IN THE SPREAD: Difficulties in certain relationships. Do not proceed with any new ventures unless you feel absolutely secure.

NEXT TO JUDGEMENT: You have undergone much pressure and it is important that you understand the lesson. Avoid any similar speculation or involvement.

FIVE OF SWORDS

KEY:
Lack of sensitivity; interested only in self gain.

MEMORY:
Too involved in selfish gain,
Lack of thought will cause great pain.

GUIDELINES:
Ruling by force does not give prolonged security.

Break-up or severing of ties; could indicate that someone has run away or left abruptly.

A chance of losing something by theft or unfair dealings.

REVERSE:
If there is no change in attitude, loss can be incurred.

MEMORY:
Let go of pride and narrow view;
Ego can inhibit you.

GUIDELINES:
Intrigue and deception involved in a personal situation.

A situation that causes all kinds of emotional problems.

Involved in an unfair decision, hard to correct at this time.

FIVE OF SWORDS

COMPARISON CHART:

YOD:
TETRAGRAMMATON = HE
PRINCIPLE = Imponderability
EXPRESSION = Son /Siva/ Neutral/Earth

HE:
ASTROLOGY = Jupiter/Taurus /Virgo/Venus/ Mercury
GNOTHOLOGY = Freedom

VAU:
SUIT KEY = Struggle & Animosity
MULTIPLE = Struggle & Effort
SIGNIFICANCE = Continual Effort & Endeavor

HE:
DIVINATION IN DEPTH:
BETWEEN FOUR AND NINE OF SWORDS: Look carefully at the spread; could signify hospitalization.

NEXT TO DEVIL: Careless spending or investment can cause financial distress.

NEXT TO MAGICIAN: Possible misuse of abilities. Don't become overconfident; you should reconsider any recent decision.

SIX OF SWORDS

KEY:
Difficult cycle now ending; allow it to phase out. Set your sights on the future, it looks good.

MEMORY:
Life moves on, just look
ahead;
Think of brighter things
instead.

GUIDELINES:
Indication of severance of a relationship.

Peace of mind and harmony will be yours, like sunshine after a storm.

Unpleasant or frustrating work situation.

Possibility of a long journey.

REVERSE KEY:
Feeling of being locked into a difficult set of circumstances. Nothing can be accomplished at this point, just wait.

MEMORY:
Difficult though your life
may be,
It will change, just wait
and see.

GUIDELINES:
Go deep within yourself and seek spiritual guidance.

Maybe it would be much wiser to think carefully; have you considered everything?

Plans, appointment or journey will be postponed.

Some re-thinking necessary.

SIX OF SWORDS

COMPARISON CHART:

YOD:
TETRAGRAMMATON = VAU
PRINCIPLE = Triality
EXPRESSION = Holy Spirit/Vishnu/Neutral/Earth

HE:
ASTROLOGY = Venus/Capricorn/Saturn
GNOTHOLOGY = Harmony

VAU:
SUIT KEY = Struggle & Animosity
MULTIPLE = Struggle & Effort
SIGNIFICANCE = Continual Effort & Endeavor

HE:
DIVINATION IN DEPTH:

ANY TEN BEFORE AND ANY TEN AFTER: Going away on a trip or to a new place of residence. Could indicate an important decision regarding a move of this nature.

NEXT TO MOON OR HIGH PRIESTESS: Wait awhile before making any changes. You don't have the full picture yet.

NEXT TO WHEEL OF FORTUNE: Expect a change in financial affairs. Don't take any unnecessary risks. Benefits are coming.

4 of Swords
7 " "
Queen of Wands
4 of " "
Hanged Man
Empress
9 of cups
10 " cups
Page of Swords
4 of Pentacles

SEVEN OF SWORDS

KEY:
Things may not work out the way you have planned.

MEMORY:
Have an alternate way to
go;
For what you wish may
not be so.

GUIDELINES:
Upset, plans not working out as expected.

One thing after another; nothing seems to be going right.

Sheer bad luck.

REVERSE KEY:
Listen carefully, someone may be offering the advice and help you need.

MEMORY:
If someone offers you
advice,
Listen well, consider
twice.

GUIDELINES:
It isn't all that bad! In fact, it isn't half as bad as you think.

You will have something returned.

Don't let false pride stand in your way.

COMPARISON CHART:

YOD:
TETRAGRAMMATON = YOD
PRINCIPLE = Substantiality
EXPRESSION = Father/Brahma/Neutral/Earth

VAU:
SUIT KEY = Struggle & Animosity
MULTIPLE = Struggle & Effort
SIGNIFICANCE = Continual Effort & Endeavor

HE:
ASTROLOGY = Sagittarius/Virgo/Mercury
GNOTHOLOGY = Wisdom — Inner Self

HE:
DIVINATION IN DEPTH:
NEXT TO FOOL: You are too changeable, flippant and inconsistent. Need to be more positive.

ALL THE SEVENS IN THE CELTIC SPREAD: Important point in your life; major cycle change, starting again under new conditions.

NEXT TO NINE OF CUPS: You will receive what you want but not necessarily in the way you want.

EIGHT OF SWORDS

KEY:
Unable to make any decision, you feel very restricted. Have experienced hurt or anxiety.

MEMORY:
Vision blocked with fear
inside;
Cannot move, you want
to hide.

GUIDELINES:
Someone concerned is both hurt and confused.

Continual worry can cause sickness; time to seek help.

Unable to think clearly, you need help and sensible advice.

REVERSE KEY:
Pressure is now being released, soon you will be free to forge ahead.

MEMORY:
Feel the ties breaking
free;
New ideas soon you'll
see.

GUIDELINES:
Soon there will be relaxation from all your tension and fears.

Pressures are now going to ease off.

The whole situation will turn around and there will be more freedom of thought and activity.

COMPARISON CHART

YOD:
TETRAGRAMMATON = HE
PRINCIPLE = Imponderability
EXPRESSION = Son/Siva/Neutral/Earth

VAU:
SUIT KEY = Struggle & Animosity
MULTIPLE = Struggle & Effort
SIGNIFICANCE = Continual Effort & Endeavor

HE:
ASTROLOGY = Capricorn/Mercury/Saturn
GNOTHOLOGY = Executive Power & Ability

HE:
DIVINATION IN DEPTH:
SWORDS ON ALL SIDES: Possibility of a health condition that needs medical attention or an operation.

NEXT TO SUN: Regardless of adverse conditions, there will be a change for the better.

NEXT TO HANGED MAN: Don't add anything, keep a quiet counsel. Don't make matters worse.

NINE OF SWORDS

KEY:
Despair and anxiety are causing misery and a sense of hopelessness.

MEMORY:
In every life comes pain
and sorrow;
But life goes on to each
tomorrow.

GUIDELINES:
Analyze the spread very carefully! Could indicate serious illness, tragedy or major operation.

Inconsolable unhappiness.

Unfortunate, sad circumstances.

REVERSE KEY:
Tomorrow holds new promise and hope.

MEMORY:
Be ready now to greet
the sun;
Be patient now, you
have won!

GUIDELINES:
Looks like good news coming!

Be patient now, blessings are coming; don't rush things.

At this time, your life tools should be faith and trust.

COMPARISON CHART:

YOD:
TETRAGRAMMATON = VAU
PRINCIPLE = Triality
EXPRESSION = Holy Spirit/Vishnu/Neutral/Earth

VAU:
SUIT KEY = Struggle & Animosity
MULTIPLE = Struggle & Effort
SIGNIFICANCE = Continual Effort & Endeavor

HE:
ASTROLOGY = Aquarius/Virgo/Taurus/Mercury/Venus
GNOTHOLOGY = Universalism

HE:
DIVINATION IN DEPTH:
NEXT TO HIGH PRIESTESS: Must be prepared to face the truth and not be afraid.

NEXT TO STAR: All is not lost, have faith and thank God for blessings already received.

ACES ON ALL SIDES: All that has happend is for the best. Look for new and beneficial beginnings.

TEN OF SWORDS

KEY:
Extreme unhappiness, depression and a deep sense of loss.

MEMORY:
All is lost, unhappiness;
Broken goals and deep
distress.

GUIDELINES:
Dreadful sense of loss; could be legal situation, job or social position.

Unfortunate collapse of plans which is difficult to accept.

Can mean separation or travel over or by water. (Check the spread and client's question to verify.)

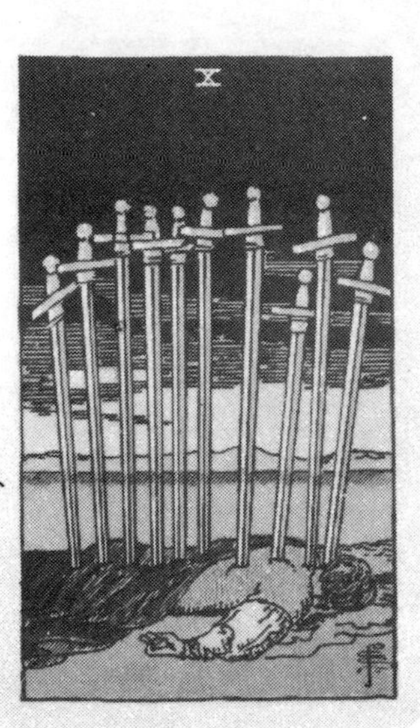

REVERSE KEY:
Cycle of events changing, coming out of a bad situation. New and positive vibrations on the way.

MEMORY:
Karmic shadow fading
now;
Need new seeds, begin
to plough.

GUIDELINES:
A Karmic lesson has now been completed.

Steady improvement in business or health.

Suffering from the aftermath of a deep personal hurt. Now in need of spiritual counselling.

COMPARISON CHART:

YOD:
TETRAGRAMMATON = HE
PRINCIPLE = Perpetuation
EXPRESSION = Nirvana/Man/Neutral/Earth

VAU:
SUIT KEY = Struggle & Animosity
MULTIPLE = Struggle & Effort
SIGNIFICANCE = Continual Effort & Endeavor

HE:
ASTROLOGY = Uranus/Taurus/Venus
GNOTHOLOGY = Individuality

HE:
DIVINATION IN DEPTH
NEXT TO EMPEROR: Difficult to understand why everything happened the way it did.

NEXT TO HERMIT: All future activities should be considered thoroughly. Need for deep thought and contemplation.

THREE FIVES IN THE CELTIC SPREAD: You are in a cycle of sudden change. Don't make plans until things are more settled.

Pentacles

A profusion of PENTACLES in a spread will generally indicate a situation involving MONEY INTERESTS.

PENTACLES SUIT KEY: MONEY INTERESTS

ACE OF PENTACLES

KEY:
Beginning of prosperity and successful ventures.

MEMORY:
At last success begins to show;
Praise comes from one you know.

GUIDELINES:
Everything's great; good foundations should bring the best results.

Could indicate receipt of a very important document or letter.

Educational degree, award or other legal document.

REVERSE KEY:
False security; great plans may not materialize.

MEMORY:
Caution now against your greed;
Be wary of someone else's need.

GUIDELINES:
Overly possessive regarding money, belongings, etc.

Maybe a wrong choice was made; follow the inner voice.

Don't be too confident, things may not work out the way you expect.

ACE OF PENTACLES

COMPARISON CHART:

YOD:
TETRAGRAMMATON = YOD
PRINCIPLE = Substantiality
EXPRESSION = Father/Brahma/Transition/Air

HE:
ASTROLOGY = Mercury/Libra/Venus
GNOTHOLOGY = Individuality

VAU:
SUIT KEY = Money Interests
MULTIPLE = Intrigue, Possible Political Activity
SIGNIFICANCE = Money & Material Needs

HE:
DIVINATION IN DEPTH:
NEXT TO SUN OR UPRIGHT WHEEL: Reaching the top! Great personal happiness in some endeavor.

LOVERS AND TEN OF CUPS IN CELTIC SPREAD: Important union, could be a major step in life. Indication of marriage plans.

THREE SWORD CARDS IN CELTIC SPREAD: Biting off more than you can chew. Consider carefully before becoming involved.

TWO OF PENTACLES

KEY:
Trying to cope with two situations, much more will be achieved if a decision is made.

MEMORY:
Shoulders broad, juggling well;
Hang in there, time will tell.

GUIDELINES:
Strong characteristics; able to cope and manage, you have stamina.

Essential that harmony is maintained; don't let change or disturbing influences perturb you.

Expect to receive acknowledgement, reassuring news, small sum of money, or gift.

REVERSE KEY:
Doubtful if plans will run smoothly, a need for more organization.

MEMORY:
Organize and change your view;
Don't give up, it's up to you.

GUIDELINES:
Disorganization is causing difficulty; you need to think of new ways.

Don't be disheartened because things are not going your way. It will straighten out.

You may receive discouraging news or information, but keep on trying.

TWO OF PENTACLES

COMPARISON CHART:

YOD:
TETRAGRAMMATON = HE
PRINCIPLE = Imponderability
EXPRESSION = Son/Siva/Transition/Air

VAU:
SUIT KEY = Money Interests
MULTIPLE = Intrigue, Possible Political Activity
SIGNIFICANCE = Money & Material Needs

HE:
ASTROLOGY = Virgo/Libra Aquarius/Venus/Uranus/Saturn
GNOTHOLOGY = Cooperation

HE:
DIVINATION IN DEPTH:

NEXT TO HANGED MAN: Don't show impatience. Wait for a situation to materialize.

NEXT TO ACE OF SWORDS: Re-evaluate any new considerations, eliminate superfluous spending, keep a tight budget.

ANY FIVE BEFORE OR AFTER: Confusion: you're scattering your energies; if you have lost something, it will be found when you settle down.

THREE OF PENTACLES

KEY:
Well informed; you have great skill, ability and talent.

MEMORY:
You can make great
progress now,
Using skills and your
know-how.

GUIDELINES:
Recognition or award for talent, ability, etc.

Indication of activities within an organization or fraternity.

Efforts will be finally rewarded; some monetary recognition.

REVERSE KEY:
Insufficient experience; you need to learn more.

MEMORY:
Keep on learning, must
know more
If in life you want to
score.

GUIDELINES:
Not the time to expect anything; more work is needed, will take a little time.

Expect a delay at this time; take it easy. Don't try to rush things.

Lack of ambition; not enough effort.

THREE OF PENTACLES

COMPARISON CHART:

YOD:

TETRAGRAMMATON = VAU
PRINCIPLE = Triality
EXPRESSION = Holy Spirit/Vishnu/Transition/Air

HE:

ASTROLOGY = Libra/Gemini/Venus/Mercury
GNOTHOLOGY = Self-expression

VAU:

SUIT KEY = Money Interests
MULTIPLE = Intrigue, Possible Political Activity
SIGNIFICANCE = Money & Material Needs

HE:

DIVINATION IN DEPTH:

NEXT TO SUN OR WHEEL OF FORTUNE: Feel secure, you're on the right path; have faith in your own talents.

THREE SWORDS IN CELTIC SPREAD: Be prepared to make a change; loss is indicated in business or some other negotiation.

NEXT TO EMPEROR: Clash of personalities in working situation. Battle of wills or disagreement.

FOUR OF PENTACLES

KEY:
Strongly attached to materialistic pursuits and endeavors.

MEMORY:
In firm command holding tight,
Doing what you feel is right.

GUIDELINES:
Fond of being in charge, likes power and will work very hard for money.

Sound judgement in business matters; has ability and well-rounded goals.

Possible receipt of gift or inheritance. (Client's question will help clarify this.)

REVERSE KEY:
Confronted with loss or obstacles.

MEMORY:
Obstacles with chance of loss;
Must establish who's the boss.

GUIDELINES:
Need to establish new plans and have them ready if confronted with obstacles.

Opposition could delay your future plans.

Indication of a spendthrift; put a halt to unnecessary spending.

FOUR OF PENTACLES

COMPARISON CHART:

YOD:
TETRAGRAMMATON = YOD
PRINCIPLE = Substantiality
EXPRESSION = Father/Brahma/ Transition/Air

HE:
ASTROLOGY = Scorpio/Aquarius/Uranus/ Saturn
GNOTHOLOGY = Self-discipline

VAU:
SUIT KEY = Money Interests
MULTIPLE = Intrigue, Possible Political Activity
SIGNIFICANCE = Money & Material Needs

HE:
DIVINATION IN DEPTH:
WHEEL OF FORTUNE AND SEVEN OF PENTACLES: Go ahead and carry out your plans. Success is all around you. Benefit from this encouraging cycle.

THREE COURT CARDS AND TOWER IN CELTIC SPREAD: Attend to your affairs and don't be influenced by others. Possibility of great loss.

NEXT TO MOON OR HIGH PRIESTESS: Undercurrents! Investigate any proposition and don't sign anything until absolutely sure.

FIVE OF PENTACLES

KEY:
Take the time to review what is happening in your life and what you want.

MEMORY:
Head too low, you cannot see
Just how good life can be.

GUIDELINES:
You may feel like throwing in the towel, but you could be on the verge of accomplishment.

Legal situation involving settlements; could mean loss.

Possibility of neglected health; more care needed.

REVERSE KEY:
Accept the Karmic lesson; try to understand your burdens.

MEMORY:
Accept the lesson, don't give in;
Admitting fault is not a sin.

GUIDELINES:
Experiencing deep spiritual need. You find it difficult to understand.

A need to show more empathy; don't let pride stand in your way.

Try to look ahead, present situation or employment may not be permanent.

FIVE OF PENTACLES

COMPARISON CHART:

YOD:

TETRAGRAMMATON = HE
PRINCIPLE = Imponderability
EXPRESSION = Son/Siva/Transition/Air

HE:

ASTROLOGY = Jupiter/Aquarius/Gemini/Uranus/Saturn/Mercury

VAU:

SUIT KEY = Money Interests
MULTIPLE = Intrigue, Possible Political Activity
SIGNIFICANCE = Money & Material Needs

HE:

DIVINATION IN DEPTH:

FOUR SWORDS IN CELTIC SPREAD: Looks like a serious dispute, severance, or losing a legal case.

NEXT TO LOVERS: Misunderstanding is causing unhappiness; could lead to a break-up in relationship.

NEXT TO NINE OR TEN OF CUPS: Signifies good luck, inheritance or other monetary gain.

SIX OF PENTACLES

KEY:
Happy atmosphere; about to enjoy the fruits of your labor.

MEMORY:
Fruits of labor now enjoy,
They could result from your employ.

GUIDELINES:
Good things happening; possible promotion, profit-sharing opportunity, or maybe a bonus.

Don't worry, you will receive what is rightfully yours.

Bread thrown on the water of life will come back threefold.

REVERSE KEY:
Unsatisfactory situation regarding the distribution of money, business, an estate, etc.

MEMORY:
Not satisfied with your share;
Disappointment seems unfair.

GUIDELINES:
Unsettled feeling; prosperity feels threatened.

Could be experiencing envy or jealousy from others.

Insecure; not being recognized for the hard work you produce.

SIX OF PENTACLES

COMPARISON CHART:

YOD:
TETRAGRAMMATON = VAU
PRINCIPLE = Triality
EXPRESSION = Holy Spirit/Vishnu/Transition/Air

HE:
ASTROLOGY = Venus/Aquarius/Libra/Uranus/Saturn
GNOTHOLOGY = Harmony

VAU:
SUIT KEY = Money Interests
MULTIPLE = Intrigue, Possible Political Activity
SIGNIFICANCE = Money & Material Needs

HE:
DIVINATION IN DEPTH:
NEXT TO STAR: Don't give up! Important to keep trying; you will be experiencing a new cycle soon.

THREE OTHER WANDS IN CELTIC SPREAD: Need to take your mind off work. Try to find some way of relaxing. Health can be affected, so slow down.

SIX ON EITHER SIDE: Harmony will soon be evident. Be content to let things take their natural course.

SEVEN OF PENTACLES

KEY:
A cycle of change that will affect your income for the better.

MEMORY:
Patient now; a cycle change
Soon your life will re-arrange.

GUIDELINES:
Growth through good honest effort and hard work.

Don't be overly anxious if in the process of negotiating money, loan or sale, etc. Plan your next move during this pause in activity.

In the process of making a major decision; there will be a welcome change in your financial situation.

REVERSE KEY:
Anxiety and depression, possibly relating to finances.

MEMORY:
Anxious thoughts create depression;
Learn all you can from this lesson.

GUIDELINES:
Feeling somewhat sorry for yourself; unable to carry on with project.

Impatience could ruin everything; don't make any rash decisions on business ventures.

Before you go ahead, think carefully. Is this what you really want?

SEVEN OF PENTACLES

COMPARISON CHART:

YOD:
TETRAGRAMMATON = YOD
PRINCIPLE = Substantiality
EXPRESSION = Father/Brahma/Transition/Air

HE:
ASTROLOGY = Sagittarius/Gemini/Mercury
GNOTHOLOGY = Wisdom — Inner Self

VAU:
SUIT KEY = Money Interests
MULTIPLE = Intrigue, Possible Political Activity
SIGNIFICANCE = Money & Material Needs

HE:
DIVINATION IN DEPTH:

NINE OF CUPS, WHEEL OF FORTUNE IN CELTIC SPREAD: Important decisions and good investments can now be made; your intuitive powers are acute at this time.

THREE SEVENS IN CELTIC SPREAD: Surrounded by many changes and opportunities; consider carefully before making a choice.

NEXT TO EMPRESS: Best not to be too critical or concerned if you do not receive instant approval from your partner.

EIGHT OF PENTACLES

KEY:
Strong characteristics; you're stable and preparing for the future.

MEMORY:
Persist and learn all you can,
And you will be the better man.

GUIDELINES:
Studying or learning a trade, skill or profession.

Not receiving much monetary gain at this time but definitely on the right track.

Dedicated to your personal goal; it seems far off, but you should persevere.

REVERSE KEY:
Going about things the wrong way; you need guidance.

MEMORY:
Shortcuts will not speed the day;
You must proceed the proper way.

GUIDELINES:
Limited ambition; too near-sighted.

Too concerned about ego, image, etc. False security. (Client's query should reveal more information.)

You want quick results, not content to work and learn in the proper manner.

EIGHT OF PENTACLES

COMPARISON CHART:

YOD:
TETRAGAMMATON = HE
PRINCIPLE = Imponderability
EXPRESSION = Son/Siva/Transition/Air

HE:
ASTROLOGY = Capricorn/Gemini/Libra/Mercury/Venus
GNOTHOLOGY = Executive Power & Ability

VAU:
SUIT KEY = Money Interests
MULTIPLE = Intrigue, Possible Political Activity
SIGNIFICANCE = Money & Material Needs

HE:
DIVINATION IN DEPTH:
FOUR PENTACLE CARDS IN CELTIC SPREAD: Increase in finances, feeling of great satisfaction.

NEXT TO FOOL: A need for caution; because everything appears to be going well, don't become careless in your work or finances.

NEXT TO HANGED MAN: Don't be afraid to pursue your goal; strike while the iron's hot.

NINE OF PENTACLES

KEY:
A feeling of being incomplete. Still seeking goals, though others may think you have it all.

MEMORY:
All seems well to those around,
But what you need you haven't found.

GUIDELINES:
Materially secure, but a feeling of solitude. Still seeking a purpose, inner satisfaction.

You are knowledgeable and handle your own affairs well.

Possible added income or receipt of money via unexpected check.

REVERSE KEY:
Time to analyze your goals and desires. Meditation may give the answer.

MEMORY:
Ask for help with your affairs;
Guidance given in your prayers.

GUIDELINES:
You may be entangled in a difficult situation. (Client's query should give indication.)

Could mean loss of friendship, partner or home, etc.

Don't make any rash decision; don't become involved in intrigues.

NINE OF PENTACLES

COMPARISON CHART:

YOD:
TETRAGRAMMATON = VAU
PRINCIPLE = Triality
EXPRESSION = Holy Spirit/Vishnu/Transition/Air

HE:
ASTROLOGY = Aquarius/Gemini/Mercury/Uranus/Saturn
GNOTHOLOGY = Universalism

VAU:
SUIT KEY = Money Interests
MULTIPLE = Intrigue, Possible Political Activity
SIGNIFICANCE = Money & Material Needs

HE:
DIVINATION IN DEPTH:
THREE SWORD CARDS IN CELTIC SPREAD: Not the time for careless spending! Keep an eye on expenses.

NEXT TO EMPEROR: Possible position of responsibility soon available. Although it will mean an increase in finances, first consider the added duties.

THREE TENS AND WORLD IN CELTIC SPREAD: A major move or long vacation. Very worthwhile.

TEN OF PENTACLES

KEY:
Beginning to feel secure but still slightly detached.

MEMORY:
Security will soon your efforts crown;
Your life will seem to turn around.

GUIDELINES:
Finances beginning to prosper; free from monetary concern.

Some gain in finances or position, possible inheritance.

Attainment or recognition; a feeling of security.

REVERSE KEY:
One problem after another! Nothing seems to gel or run smoothly.

MEMORY:
Lost and don't know what to do;
Problems seem to stick to you.

GUIDELINES:
Problems concerning money: could be will, pension, wages, etc.

Lethargic, bored, not doing anything, you can be persuaded to go in the wrong direction unless you become self-motivated.

Upset caused by someone close. Be objective and take command of the situation.

COMPARISON CHART:

YOD:
TETRAGRAMMATON = HE
PRINCIPLE = Perpetuation
EXPRESSION = Man/Nirvana/Transition/Air

VAU:
SUIT KEY = Money Interests
MULTIPLE = Intrigue, Possible Political Activity
SIGNIFICANCE = Money & Material Needs

HE:
ASTROLOGY = Uranus/Aquarius/Saturn
GNOTHOLOGY = Individuality

HE:
DIVINATION IN DEPTH:
NEXT TO SUN OR WORLD: Fulfillment and true happiness.

NEXT TO LOVERS WITH ACE OF CUPS IN CELTIC SPREAD: Celebration, union, joy.

DEVIL AND TOWER WITH TWO ACE CARDS IN CELTIC SPREAD: Upset, could be problem with business, career, etc. Other people involved; need to make fresh plans and a new start.

CHAPTER 8
THE COURT MENTORS

Symbology

KING represents MAN in his maturity.
QUEEN represents WOMAN in her maturity.
KNIGHT represents YOUNG MAN.
PAGE represents YOUNG BOY or GIRL, or CHILD of either sex.

Coloring

WANDS = Fair hair/red hair, blue eyes, fair skin.
CUPS = Light to medium brown hair, hazel eyes, medium skin.
SWORDS = Dark brown/black hair, dark eyes, olive skin.
PENTACLES = White hair, any color eyes, fair skin. Can also represent members of the dark-skinned races.

Suit Keys

WANDS = Enterprise and distinction.
CUPS = Love and happiness.
SWORDS = Struggle and animosity
PENTACLES = Money interests.

NOTE: COURT CARDS usually represent PEOPLE, but can also represent SITUATIONS. The client's query, the complete Tarot spread and the wisdom of the Tarot being sought by the reader will determine which is appropriate in each situation.

KING OF WANDS

KEY:
A man secure in business or profession. Strong and generous, can be impulsive.

MEMORY:
Fair hair, red hair, eyes of blue;
Generous, strong, impulsive, too.

GUIDELINES:
Man in his maturity.

Likelihood of unexpected money.

Excellent leadership qualities which should be channeled in the right direction.

Take your time in any upcoming agreement before making a final decision.

REVERSE KEY:
A man inclined to be intolerant and strict in his manner. Could be opposing the client.

MEMORY:
Eyes of blue, hair red and fair;
Disagreement you can share.

GUIDELINES:
Man in his maturity.

Indication of a disagreement or dispute. Be the first to withdraw.

You may feel uneasy through lack of tolerance in a business concern.

Be sure that all the facts are correct; don't allow anyone to be overly aggressive with you.

COMPARISON CHART:

YOD:
TETRAGRAMMATON = YOD
PRINCIPLE = Substantiality
EXPRESSION = Father/Brahma/Active/Fire

HE:
ASTROLOGY = Aries Disposition
GNOTHOLOGY = Individuality

VAU:
SUIT KEY = Enterprise & Distinction
MULTIPLE = Indicate Change
SIGNIFICANCE = Business & Success

HE:
DIVINATION IN DEPTH:
MANY COURT CARDS IN SPREAD: Indicate many people involved in the situation.

MANY WANDS IN SPREAD: Indicate movement, activities, change.

QUEEN OF WANDS

KEY:
Woman who has an attractive personality and draws people to her.

MEMORY:
Fair hair, red hair, eyes of blue;
Loves her home and nature too.

GUIDELINES:
Woman in her maturity.

Has a sensible attitude and can be most helpful with good advice.

If either Page, Knight or King is next to her in the spread, she is usually connected with one of them.

Don't be afraid to ask this lady for assistance; she will help if she can.

REVERSE KEY:
Woman who is inclined to be rather narrow-minded. Often takes a domineering approach.

MEMORY:
Eyes of blue, hair red and fair;
Frivolous ways she cannot bear.

GUIDELINES:
Woman in her maturity.

Exceptionally strict and can be unbending.

Indicaton of unfaithfulness in some relationship; check other cards in the spread.

Avoid confiding in a woman who may feel bitter at this time.

COMPARISON CHART:

YOD:
TETRAGRAMMATON = HE
PRINCIPLE = Imponderability
EXPRESSION = Son/Siva/Active/Fire

HE:
ASTROLOGY = Leo Disposition
GNOTHOLOGY = Cooperation

VAU:
SUIT KEY = Enterprise & Distinction
MULTIPLE = Indicate Change
SIGNIFICANCE = Business & Success

HE:

DIVINATION IN DEPTH:
MANY COURT CARDS IN SPREAD: Indicate many people involved in the situation.

MANY WANDS IN SPREAD: Indicate movement, activities, change.

KNIGHT OF WANDS

KEY:
Young man can create vibrations that will call for sudden decisions or change in life.

MEMORY:
Fair hair, red hair, eyes of blue;
Young man's views may trouble you.

GUIDELINES:
Young man.

Expect someone to present thoughts or ideas pertaining to business which will be advantageous.

The start or finish of an important situation; spread will determine.

Journey by water or over water; also possible change of residence.

REVERSE KEY:
You feel restricted by minor disputes. Young man possible cause.

MEMORY:
Eyes of blue, hair red and fair;
Indecision in the air.

GUIDELINES:
Young man.

Lack of energy, despondent; you should be encouraged to try something new.

Frustration and indecision; you should follow your conscience and act accordingly.

Jealousy is causing odd behavior.

COMPARISON CHART:

YOD:
TETRAGRAMMATON = VAU
PRINCIPLE = Triality
EXPRESSION = Holy Spirit/Vishnu/Active/Fire

VAU:
SUIT KEY = Enterprise & Distinction
MULTIPLE = Indicate Change
SIGNIFICANCE = Business & Success

HE:
ASTROLOGY = Gemini Disposition
GNOTHOLOGY = Self expression

HE:
DIVINATION IN DEPTH:
MANY COURT CARDS IN SPREAD: Indicate many people involved in the situation.

MANY WANDS IN SPREAD: Indicate movement, activities, change.

PAGE OF WANDS

KEY:
Indication of message from a near relative or close friend.

REVERSE KEY:
Receiving information from a young person.

MEMORY:
Fair hair, red hair, eyes of blue;
Someone young has news for you.

MEMORY:
Eyes of blue, hair red and fair;
Information will soon be there.

GUIDELINES:
Young boy, girl or child.

Happy news on the way.

Possible letter or telephone call that will please you.

GUIDELINES:
Young boy, girl or child.

Uncomfortable relationship with person who is domineering.

Someone could be upsetting you.

COMPARISON CHART:

YOD:
TETRAGRAMMATON = HE
PRINCIPLE = Perpetuation
EXPRESSION = Nirvana/Man/Active/Fire

HE:
ASTROLOGY = Sagittarius Disposition
GNOTHOLOGY = Self-discipline

VAU:
SUIT KEY = Enterprise & Distinction
MULTIPLE = Indicate Change
SIGNIFICANCE = Business & Success

HE:
DIVINATION IN DEPTH:
MANY COURT CARDS IN SPREAD: Indicate many people involved in the situation.

MANY WANDS IN SPREAD: Indicate movement, activities change.

KING OF CUPS

KEY:
A reliable, repected man from any walk of life. He is trustworthy and can help you.

MEMORY:
Light brown hair, blue-hazel eyes;
This good man is very wise.

GUIDELINES:
Man in his maturity.

Man with much empathy who could provide wise counselling.

Quiet type of man who keeps his emotions hidden.

Could be in the Church, a teacher or associated with law.

REVERSE KEY:
Avoid entanglement, this man is not always what he appears to be.

MEMORY:
Blue-hazel eyes, hair light to brown;
Powerful man can put you down.

GUIDLINES:
Man in his maturity.

Indication of double-dealing or loss; could be person or situation. Check the cards in the spread for confirmation.

You may feel you have been treated badly and misled.

Avoid disagreement; better to find your own solution.

COMPARISON CHART:

YOD:
TETRAGRAMMATON = YOD
PRINCIPLE = Substantiality
EXPRESSION = Father/Brahma/Passive/Water

HE:
ASTROLOGY = Cancer Disposition
GNOTHOLOGY = Individuality

VAU:
SUIT KEY = Love & Happiness
MULTIPLE = Love & Emotions
SIGNIFICANCE = Joy & Affection

HE:

DIVINATION IN DEPTH:
MANY COURT CARDS IN SPREAD: Indicate many people involved in the situation.

MANY CUPS IN SPREAD: Loved ones, deep emotions and concerns.

QUEEN OF CUPS

KEY:
Sensitive lady who relies on her intuitive ability rather than common sense.

MEMORY:
Light brown hair, blue-
hazel eyes;
On intuition she relies.

GUIDELINES:
Woman in her maturity.

Lady with perception, can see ahead and believe.

Awaited pleasures and success are now coming due.

Can be difficult to approach but will help you when her confidence is won.

REVERSE KEY:
This lady can present a good story, is intelligent but inclined to exaggerate. Means well but not fully reliable.

MEMORY:
Blue-hazel eyes, hair
light to brown;
Embellishment is her
crown.

GUIDELINES:
Woman in her maturity.

Lacks depth; unwise to relate any secrets to her.

Indication that someone is being deceived, or that you are not aware of the whole situation.

Go elsewhere at this time for any further discussion regarding a confidence; this person does not have the sympathy or understanding that you think she has.

COMPARISON CHART:
YOD:
TETRAGRAMMATON = HE
PRINCIPLE = Imponderability
EXPRESSION = Son/Siva/Passive/Water

VAU:
SUIT KEY = Love & Happiness
MULTIPLE = Love & Emotions
SIGNIFICANCE = Joy & Affection

HE:
ASTROLOGY = Scorpio Disposition
GNOTHOLOGY = Cooperation

HE:
DIVINATION IN DEPTH:
MANY COURT CARDS IN SPREAD: Indicate many people involved in the situation.

MANY CUPS IN SPREAD: Loved ones, deep emotions and concerns.

KNIGHT OF CUPS

KEY:
Young man can offer interesting invitations or proposals.

MEMORY:
Light brown hair, blue hazel eyes;
Tempting offer can cause ties.

GUIDELINES:
Young man.

Someone you love may have an opposing view; this can present difficulty.

Intelligent young man with artistic flair, interesting to be with.

A deep relationship with Karmic ties.

REVERSE KEY:
If you have received an unusual offer, it's advisable to check circumstances before accepting.

MEMORY:
Blue-hazel eyes, hair light to brown;
After smiles, you may frown.

GUIDELINES:
Young man.

Look before you leap! Get the whole picture.

Don't be put off by imaginative stories. Half truths can promote difficulties in a relationship.

Before any papers are signed, check with a third party.

COMPARISON CHART:

YOD:
TETRAGRAMMATON = VAU
PRINCIPLE = Triality
EXPRESSION = Holy Spirit/Vishnu/Passive/Water

VAU:
SUIT KEY = Love & Happiness
MULTIPLE = Love & Emotions
SIGNIFICANCE = Joy & Affection

HE:
ASTROLOGY = Sagittarius Disposition
GNOTHOLOGY = Self-expression

HE:
DIVINATION IN DEPTH:
MANY COURT CARDS IN SPREAD: Indicate many people involved in the situation.

MANY CUPS IN SPREAD: Loved ones, deep emotions and concerns.

PAGE OF CUPS

KEY:
Young person who can offer help or cooperation; a gentle and quiet person.

MEMORY:
Light brown hair, blue-
hazel eyes;
A gentle soul brings a
surprise.

GUIDELINES:
Young boy, girl or child.

Can mean news of a birth or a wonderful idea, plan or program.

Important message arriving.

Be ready to start a new project.

REVERSE KEY:
You will be offered help, possibly by a young person or through his concern.

MEMORY:
Hazel eyes could be blue;
Hair light to brown will
comfort you.

GUIDELINES:
Young boy, girl or child.

Obstacles will soon be removed and you will see things in a new light.

Lethargic, not much desire to plan ahead.

Things are changing; don't dwell on yesterday.

COMPARISON CHART:

YOD:
TETRAGRAMMATON = HE
PRINCIPLE = Perpetuation
EXPRESSION = Nirvana/Man/Passive/Water

HE:
ASTROLOGY = Pisces Disposition
GNOTHOLOGY = Self-discipline

VAU:
SUIT KEY = Love & Happiness
MULTIPLE = Love & Emotions
SIGNIFICANCE = Joy & Affection

HE:
MANY COURT CARDS IN SPREAD: Indicate many people involved in the situation.

MANY CUPS IN SPREAD: Loved ones, deep emotions and concerns.

KING OF SWORDS

KEY:
This man has authority, could be with the government or associated with law. He gives excellent counsel.

MEMORY:
Hair brown to black and
eyes so dark;
His advice hits the mark.

GUIDELINES:
Man in his maturity.

You will find this man to be most reliable; take his advice.

You can be mistaken about the attitude of this man; he is cautious and thinks before committing himself.

Could represent a man with an official title, civilian or military.

REVERSE KEY:
This man's personality is inclined to be strict to the point of cruelty. He does not appear to have any compassion.

MEMORY:
Dark eyes, hair black or
brown;
Travel fast when he's
around.

GUIDELINES:
Man in his maturity.

This man can be a bully and upsets people easily.

May represent an extremely stern father, husband, partner.

Indication of injustice, unfairness and adamant decision.

COMPARISON CHART:

YOD:
TETRAGRAMMATON = YOD
PRINCIPLE = Substantiality
EXPRESSION = Father/Brahma/Neutral/Earth

VAU:
SUIT KEY = Struggle & Animosity
MULTIPLE = Struggle & Effort
SIGNIFICANCE = Continual Effort & Endeavor

HE:
ASTROLOGY = Taurus Disposition
GNOTHOLOGY = Individuality

HE:
DIVINATION IN DEPTH:
MANY COURT CARDS IN SPREAD: Indicate many people involved in the situation.

MANY SWORDS IN SPREAD: Indicate strife, pressures and concerns.

QUEEN OF SWORDS

KEY:
Lady with sharp wit who appears to have money. Could be a widow or divorced. Probably does not have children.

MEMORY:
Hair brown to black and
eyes so dark;
Wit so quick it lights a
spark.

GUIDELINES:
Woman in her maturity.

A serious and good counsellor who can give the right kind of help.

Spiritual depth caused by prolonged struggle.

Difficult to keep up with the many demands of life.

REVERSE KEY:
This lady can be intolerant, with a narrow outlook on life. She finds it difficult to see anyone else's point of view.

MEMORY:
Dark eyes, hair black or
brown;
When you're up, she'll
put you down.

GUIDELINES:
Woman in her maturity.

This woman enjoys gossip; unwise to confide in her.

Her perception is keen but she can be deceiving; you should learn to ignore the opinions of this lady.

Often this lady is not understood and can deceive people.

COMPARISON CHART:

YOD:
TETRAGRAMMATON = HE
PRINCIPLE = Imponderability
EXPRESSION = Son/Siva/Neutral/Earth

VAU:
SUIT KEY = Struggle & Animosity
MULTIPLE = Struggle & Effort
SIGNIFICANCE = Continual Effort & Endeavor

HE:
ASTROLOGY = Virgo Disposition
GNOTHOLOGY = Cooperation

HE:
DIVINATION IN DEPTH:
MANY COURT CARDS IN SPREAD: Indicate many people involved in the situation.

MANY SWORDS IN SPREAD: Indicate strife, pressures and concerns.

KNIGHT OF SWORDS

KEY:
Courteous young man has good intentions but his attitude can be overbearing.

MEMORY:
Hair brown to black and
eyes so dark;
Gallant ventures will
embark.

GUIDELINES:
Young man.

You can expect to feel the strength of this young man, which will help considerably.

You are going through a difficult period; check the spread for more details.

Someone favors you and will defend you and promote good vibrations.

REVERSE KEY:
Steer clear of this young man; he could upset your plans and create trouble.

MEMORY:
Dark eyes, hair black or
brown;
Can turn your plans upside down.

GUIDELINES:
Young man.

Someone is opposed to your thoughts or plans.

Not a good time to start any new projects or changes in life style.

Wait a little longer before going ahead; patience will make you a winner.

COMPARISON CHART:

YOD:
TETRAGRAMMATON = VAU
PRINCIPLE = Triality
EXPRESSION = Holy Spirit/Vishnu/Neutral/Earth

VAU:
SUIT KEY = Struggle & Animosity
MULTIPLE = Struggle & Effort
SIGNIFICANCE = Continual Effort & Endeavor

HE:
ASTROLOGY = Aries Disposition
GNOTHOLOGY = Self-discipline

HE:
DIVINATION IN DEPTH:
MANY COURT CARDS IN SPREAD: Indicate many people involved in the situation.

MANY SWORDS IN SPREAD: Indicate strife, pressures and concerns.

PAGE OF SWORDS

KEY:
A young person's activities could be causing you some concern.

MEMORY:
Hair brown to black and eyes so dark;
Energetic person, on the mark!

GUIDELINES:
Young boy, girl or child.

Someone is definitely on the defensive.

You may not like the possible delay in plans.

Could indicate news you will consider disappointing.

REVERSE KEY:
Young people are sometimes unpredictable; be prepared for the unexpected.

MEMORY:
Dark eyes, hair black or brown,
Can cause you to think or frown.

GUIDELINES:
Young boy, girl or child.

You should look further into the situation to fully understand.

Could indicate someone feeling sick; look to other cards in the spread for more information.

Eventually the change will be more beneficial.

COMPARISON CHART:

YOD:
TETRAGRAMMATON = HE
PRINCIPLE = Perpetuation
EXPRESSION = Nirvana/Man/Neutral/Earth

HE:
ASTROLOGY = Capricorn Disposition
GNOTHOLOGY = Self-discipline

VAU:
SUIT KEY = Struggle & Animosity
MULTIPLE = Struggle & Effort
SIGNIFICANCE = Continual Effort & Endeavor

HE:
DIVINATION IN DEPTH:
MANY COURT CARDS IN SPREAD: Indicate many people involved in the situation.

MANY SWORDS IN SPREAD: Indicate strife, pressures and concerns.

KING OF PENTACLES

KEY:
Good position in industry; this man is competent in mathematical procedures, a generous soul who is friendly and affectionate.

MEMORY:
Hair so white or dark as night;
His calculations always right.

GUIDELINES:
Man in his maturity.

Banker, investor or large property owner.

Solid and steady; could be of great help.

Gifted man, not overcome by his position in life.

REVERSE KEY:
This man is most materialistic, talks a lot and often appears stupid. He is opinionated and easily led.

MEMORY:
White hair, dark hair, any race;
His opinions are quite base.

GUIDELINES:
Man in his maturity.

Not too difficult to bribe this man.

Skims the surface of everything; perverse use of talents and ability.

Usually oblivious to negative remarks but can display great anger if aroused.

COMPARISON CHART:

YOD:
TETRAGRAMMATON = YOD
PRINCIPLE = Substantiality
EXPRESSION = Father/Brahma/Transition/Air

HE:
ASTROLOGY = Gemini Disposition
GNOTHOLOGY = Individuality

VAU:
SUIT KEY = Money Interests
MULTIPLE = Intrigue, Disguised Activities
SIGNIFICANCE = Money & Material Needs

HE:
DIVINATION IN DEPTH:
MANY COURT CARDS IN SPREAD: Indicate many people involved in the situation.

MANY PENTACLES IN SPREAD: Monetary transactions, banking, lending, borrowing, etc.

QUEEN OF PENTACLES

KEY:
A creative lady with many talents, family oriented and charitable.

MEMORY:
Hair so white or dark as night;
Will help someone in a plight.

GUIDELINES:
Woman in her maturity.

Can be a great business woman; is not afraid of hard work.

Tends to become despondent and can retire inwards.

At her best she is able to use her talents well and be happy at work or at home.

REVERSE KEY:
This lady finds it difficult to trust anyone. Insecurity causes a suspicious nature.

MEMORY:
White hair, dark hair, any race;
Ignores things she cannot face.

GUIDELINES:
Woman in her maturity.

Too much dependence on others, inclined to be lazy.

Fear of failing makes this lady quite changeable; she lacks motivation.

Often this lady will neglect her responsibilities because of insecurity.

COMPARISON CHART:

YOD:
TETRAGRAMMATON = HE
PRINCIPLE = Imponderability
EXPRESSION = Son/Siva/Transition/Air

HE:
ASTROLOGY = Libra Disposition
GNOTHOLOGY = Cooperation

VAU:
SUIT KEY = Money Interests
MULTIPLE = Intrigue, Disguised Activities
SIGNIFICANCE = Money & Material Needs

HE:
DIVINATION IN DEPTH:
MANY COURT CARDS IN SPREAD: Indicate many people involved in the situation.

MANY PENTACLES IN SPREAD: Monetary transactions, banking, lending, borrowing, etc.

KNIGHT OF PENTACLES

KEY:
This young man is thorough and will take the time to do a good job.

MEMORY:
Hair so white or dark as night;
Sets his goals at lofty height.

GUIDELINES:
Young man.

Trustworthy, will not experiment outside his goal. Can give the wrong impression.

A love for animals and nature; could make an excellent veterinarian.

Needs constant motivation, otherwise his outlook may become subdued and he may waste his talents.

Good worker and has empathy with those less fortunate.

REVERSE KEY:
An irresponsible and impatient attitude affects the progress of this young man.

MEMORY:
White hair, dark hair, any race;
Fails too often through his haste.

GUIDELINES:
Young man.

Money, work and other important matters seem to be at a standstill.

Needs lots of encouragement, tends to be timid and make mistakes.

Received some hard knocks in his life, needs the security of love.

Dissatisfied with everything and everyone, looking for a new start.

COMPARISON CHART:

YOD:
TETRAGRAMMATON = VAU
PRINCIPLE = Triality
EXPRESSION = Holy Spirit/Vishnu/Transition/Air

VAU:
SUIT KEY = Money Interests
MULTIPLE = Intrigue, Disguised Activities
SIGNIFICANCE = Money & Material Needs

HE:
ASTROLOGY = Taurus Disposition
GNOTHOLOGY = Self-expression

HE:
DIVINATION IN DEPTH:
MANY COURT CARDS IN SPREAD: Indicate many people involved in the situation.

MANY PENTACLES IN SPREAD: Monetary transactions, banking, lending, borrowing, etc.

PAGE OF PENTACLES

KEY:
A young person who enjoys studying and is a persevering scholar.

MEMORY:
Hair so white or dark as night;
Can usually help to put things right.

GUIDELINES:
Young boy, girl or child.

A person will be giving you good news that will change many things.

A meeting with someone who is kind and generous, sympathetic to your point of view.

Changes for the better caused by someone who cares.

REVERSE KEY:
A quiet young person; can be moody but is goal-oriented

MEMORY:
White hair, dark hair, any race;
Studies well in every phase.

GUIDELINES:
Young boy, girl or child.

Your views are not appreciated by those around you.

Materialistic, love of luxury and comfort.

Unfavorable news; don't be rebellious.

COMPARISON CHART:

YOD:
TETRAGRAMMATON = HE
PRINCIPLE = Perpetuation
EXPRESSION = Nirvana/Man Transition/Air

VAU:
SUIT KEY = Money Interests
MULTIPLE = Intrigue, Possible Political Activity
SIGNIFICANCE = Money & Material Needs

HE:
ASTROLOGY = Aquarius Disposition
GNOTHOLOGY = Self-discipline

HE:
DIVINATION IN DEPTH:
MANY COURT CARDS IN SPREAD: Indicate many people involved in the situation.

MANY PENTACLES IN SPREAD: Monetary transactions, banking, lending, borrowing, etc.

CHAPTER 9
THE MAJOR MENTORS

The Major Arcana

0 THE FOOL
1 THE MAGICIAN
2 THE HIGH PRIESTESS
3 THE EMPRESS
4 THE EMPEROR
5 THE HIEROPHANT
6 THE LOVERS
7 THE CHARIOT
8 STRENGTH
9 THE HERMIT
10 WHEEL OF FORTUNE
11 JUSTICE
12 THE HANGED MAN
13 DEATH
14 TEMPERANCE
15 THE DEVIL
16 THE TOWER
17 THE STAR
18 THE MOON
19 THE SUN
20 JUDGEMENT
21 THE WORLD

0 THE FOOL

KEY:
You are now at the crossroads; the decision you make can be important, think carefully.

MEMORY:
You have the power to use your will;
Choose with wisdom, be soul-still.

GUIDELINES:
Past mistakes could be the best lesson; look before you leap.

Any indiscretion at this time could spoil everything.

The best swimmer in the world must know the depth before he makes his dive.

REVERSE KEY:
Have you made the right choice? You could be wrong. If discontented or lacking in motivation, why not review things to date?

MEMORY:
If discontent is all you know,
Check back; in time it will show.

GUIDELINES:
Whatever is causing concern, don't brood about it, have the courage to discuss it.

Be strong and listen to your inner voice; don't listen to others at this time.

Before you make your next move, are you happy with things so far?

0 THE FOOL

COMPARISON CHART:

YOD:

TETRAGRAMMATON = HE = YOD

PRINCIPLE = Substantiality

EXPRESSION = Father/Creator/God/Intellectual/Active

HE:

ASTROLOGY = Pluto

GNOTHOLOGY = Master Vibration 33

VAU:

MEDITATION:

Each precious day we can begin our journey like the Fool, completely untouched by any event the day may bring and by any emotions. Fearing nothing, we trust God implicitly, knowing full well we are divinely guided and always protected. Feel the fresh innocence of this God-like soul, free to go wherever he desires. Try to understand how he is totally filled with the Holy Spirit. Free of fear, he truly knows himself and values the experiences of all his past existence. Listen to his song: "The Lord is my Shepherd, I shall not want."

TIME:

Before your day begins, before apprehension puts its yoke upon you. This early meditation can fill your day with new courage and childlike happiness. Be prepared to start the day with "You" and not the fears of yesterday. This will truly help you to "know thyself."

HE:

SEPHIROTH = Triad of Intelligence

PATH = Chochma to Kether

HEBREW = Aleph

ENGLISH = Ox

1 THE MAGICIAN

KEY:
Know that everything is possible through the power of God.

MEMORY:
Through God's love let
all men know
All is given, blessings
flow.

GUIDELINES:
Application of will and the courage to have faith is the formula for success.

You are well blessed and your fervent attitude will bring about what you need.

You are going in the right direction.

REVERSE KEY:
Abuse of power, the ability to manipulate words and actions to suit your own selfish needs.

MEMORY:
Hidden truths and cunning ways
Can hurt your life in
coming days.

GUIDELINES:
Not applying yourself in the right way; cannot achieve anything unless you change your attitude.

Lack of willpower, cannot seem to cope with obstacles. Too busy finding the easy way out.

Undercurrents, possible deceit, not telling the whole story. You should look deeper into the situation.

1 THE MAGICIAN

COMPARISON CHART:

YOD:
TETRAGAMMATON = YOD
PRINCIPLE = Substantiality
EXPRESSION = Father/Creator/God/Intellectual/Active

HE:
ASTROLOGY = Mercury
GNOTHOLOGY = Individuality

VAU:

MEDITATION:

You must learn to go within yourself and use the divine power available. Life presents opportunities that are not always recognized because they are offered in the embryonic state. He who does not understand the divine wisdom sees only the mighty oak and ignores the potential of the acorn. Through the wisdom of the Tarot, we battle with seeds that have remained undernourished through lack of recognition. It is easy to learn that Cups represent Love and Happiness, but the sensitive Tarot Master is able to detect the SEED of love in the thimble, the beginnings of negative vibrations in the penknife. Man must know himself, he must know his desires by laying them openly on the table of life and believing that all is possible to those who have faith. Make known your request to God and reach out to the divine channel for His promised manifestations.

TIME:

At least one hour after rising, to enable you to see clearly your true desires and goals. Know that you are an instrument of God and bring down the divine power.

HE:
SEPHIROTH = Triad of Intelligence
PATH = 12—Binah to Kether
HEBREW = Beth
ENGLISH = House

2 THE HIGH PRIESTESS

KEY:
Activity beneath the surface; the whole picture cannot be seen at this point. Much depth.

MEMORY:
Behind the veil, within your grasp,
Living knowledge from the past.

GUIDELINES:
Ability to use intuition and receive spiritual inspiration.

Best to keep your intentions or ideas to yourself. Be sure to select the right person for any confidence shared.

Be yourself in any situation; have complete faith in your feelings at this time.

REVERSE KEY:
Superficial situation; there are no secret acitivities involved.

MEMORY:
Nothing hidden, naught to fear;
All is seen, don't waste a tear.

GUIDELINES:
At this point examine everything, do not place trust until you have completely analyzed the situation.

Can refer to a person with weak character and lacking in stamina. Could affect a relationship or any kind of support you may be needing.

Suggests a complete review of person or situation; strength is lacking, need for a deeper commitment.

2 THE HIGH PRIESTESS

COMPARISON CHART:

YOD:
TETRAGRAMMATON = HE
PRINCIPLE = Imponderability
EXPRESSION = Son/ Receiver/ Man/Moral/ Passive

HE:
ASTROLOGY = Virgo
GNOTHOLOGY = Cooperation

VAU:

MEDITATION:

The student who is aware of his own "self-made" obstacles can find enlightenment through meditation on this beautiful Tarot symbol. Through sincere effort and concentration, you can remove the barrier between your inner and outer being. Upon achieving this level of tranquility, you will be aware only of One Divine Consciousness, which in turn will reveal your original soul journey and throw light upon your original goals. You will rid yourself of inhibitions and all earthy fears and become motivated by standards you thought impossible. Upon reaching the inner center of soul activity, the mysteries once hidden deep within the superconscious will come to the surface and reveal your destiny. So often we feel inadequate, not knowing which way is best, but having attained peace of mind, we can sit serene like the High Priestess, recognizing the constant flow of both negative and positive vibrations and accepting the conditions around us. Look into the power of your subconscious and bravely make the change that will heal your soul and body.

TIME:

This is a beautiful evening meditation. Allow time afterwards to contemplate the beauty and strength of truly being at ONE with yourself. Peace is granted to the soul who goes to sleep in tune with God.

HE:
SEPHIROTH = Triad of Intelligence
PATH = 13—Tiphares to Kether
HEBREW = Gimel
ENGLISH = Camel

3 THE EMPRESS

KEY:
Promise of growth, prosperity and fertility in all things. Needs fulfilled with joy and satisfaction.

MEMORY:
Health, children and business good;
All is well, you knew you could.

GUIDELINES:
Original seeds were well planted, harvest is wonderful. Now is the time to reap the benefits.

The results or gains are much larger than anticipated. Look forward to a happy conclusion.

Coming to the end and completion of hard work and sacrifice. Soon recognition and rewards will come for your efforts.

REVERSE KEY:
Wasteful energies causing despair and failure. Unproductive activity can affect home and income.

MEMORY:
All looks black, the reason why:
You built castles in the sky.

GUIDELINES:
Affairs are not coordinated, chaotic situations are arising. A need for good counsel and advice.

Someone is suffering and feels the pangs of poverty or inability to meet obligations; could be suffering financially and unable to make ends meet.

Depressing vibrations make you feel empty and withdrawn. Unable to understand the trials and pain endured. Feeling of hopelessness, throwing in the towel.

3 THE EMPRESS

COMPARISON CHART:

YOD:

TETRAGRAMMATON = VAU
PRINCIPLE = Triality
EXPRESSION = Spirit/Transformer/Universe/Material/Neutral

HE:

ASTROLOGY = Libra
GNOTHOLOGY = Self-expression

VAU:

MEDITATION:

To fully understand the female principle and evolutionary process, we must realize that the mystery of woman and her ability to produce children is unique and God-given. We must learn to appreciate the qualities of motherhood and how the strength of the female relates to earthly responsibilities. Woman plays a remarkable role in nature: it is through her that man is born. The Empress in all her feminine glory fulfills every man's dreams and hopes. We should attempt to study her earthly role and feel the essence of life pulsate in every living thing. Know the majestic splendor of continual reproduction in the whole concept of nature. Experience the throb of Divinity in every growing thing. Learn to listen to the constant cry of mankind reaching out to touch its destiny. Through each other, man and woman should find peace and harmony. Meditation on this vibrant symbol will teach us the true purpose of life. We must understand that the Empress does not represent the female alone; in her hidden symbols the program of life is a haunting melody of continual fulfillment. The pure joy of this beautiful symbol is in all of us. It is awakened by our mother and completed through our mate or partner. True love is being in perfect harmony with the universal heartbeat, finding in each other the glory of the Father.

TIME:

Early morning or early evening, when the earth is in the process of changing and giving us her many blessings.

HE:

SEPHIROTH = Triad of Intelligence
PATH = 14 — Binah — Chochma
HEBREW = Daleth
ENGLISH = Door

4 THE EMPEROR

KEY:
Balance and authority, mind over matter, experience and knowledge.

MEMORY:
Truth and justice known within;
Forgiveness means admitting sin.

GUIDELINES:
A controlled person who relies on his own intellect, not easily influenced.

Someone who is well respected and holds a position of authority.

Can indicate versatile abilities; important to retain inner balance.

REVERSE KEY:
Positive direction is needed, lack of control, need for self-discipline.

MEMORY:
Butterfly flits and knows no way;
Man must plan and work each day.

GUIDELINES:
Possible that you are feeling the weight of responsiblity; someone is becoming a burden.

Someone could be after something you have. Be sure you understand the motives of this person.

Do not tolerate anyone who does not appear to be self-sufficient; he can become a great responsibility.

4 THE EMPEROR

COMPARISON CHART:

YOD:

TETRAGRAMMATON = HE = YOD
PRINCIPLE = Substantiality
EXPRESSION = Father/Creator/God/Intellectual/Active

HE:

ASTROLOGY = Scorpio
GNOTHOLOGY = Self-discipline

VAU:

MEDITATION:

As we go into meditation with the Emperor, we need to explore the order of the higher planes and to learn how discipline affects law and order here on earth. Only by aspiring to a higher and keener development of spiritual law can we begin to accept the divine principles here in our materialistic world. On reflection we can see that the balance of man is only disturbed when he is not in tune with the necessary order of things. When man allows his life cycle to become entirely dependent on earthly things, he becomes isolated and is aware of spiritual friction; in this predicament he resorts to his basic emotions and blames others for the mess he is personally responsible for. Bitterness is the result, and we can easily become sour critics and slowly burn away the life-giving forces with anger and unhappinesss. Our goal in this meditation is to reach out to the source of heavenly perfection and to learn why the natural laws are important to each individual. We must learn to be grateful for the strict discipline of the heavens and endeavor to bring the same balance into our own lives. Clarity of soul awaits the man who keeps the divine law and also abides by man's law.

TIME:

In a closed environment with gentle light; perhaps a candle. In this soft, enclosed atmosphere you can be receptive to the laws of the universe. Leadership is necessary for man, and if you are wise, leadership will come naturally. If you are merely a follower, it is only because you chose to be.

HE:

SEPHIROTH = Triad of Intelligence
PATH = 28-Yesod — Netzach
HEBREW = Tzaddi
ENGLISH = Fishhook

5 THE HIEROPHANT

KEY:
He who conforms and diligently searches for truth must recognize that he himself is not truth.

MEMORY:
You are right, according
to Hoyle;
Others' mistakes make
your blood boil.

GUIDELINES:
A nice person in a lot of ways, but can be stubborn and exasperating.

A solid organization, establishment or system. Not open to any changes.

Someone who prefers to belong for the sake of belonging. Outside appearances are important, likes to impress.

REVERSE KEY:
A keen sense of originality; one who is not afraid to undertake new ventures or explore and has an open mind.

MEMORY:
Free spirit glows within
your soul;
New adventures make
you whole.

GUIDELINES:
Possibility of someone who will listen to new ideas, programs, etc.

Don't be afraid to speak your mind; do what you feel is best. Go ahead and have the courage of your convictions.

A new and refreshing vibration coming into your life. Can denote openmindedness and a frank outlook on life.

5 THE HIEROPHANT

COMPARISON CHART:

YOD:

TETRAGRAMMATON = HE
PRINCIPLE = Imponderability
EXPRESSION = Son/Receiver /Man/Moral/ Passive

HE:

ASTROLOGY = Jupiter
GNOTHOLOGY = Freedom

VAU:

MEDITATION:

This prayer of meditation will uplift you to higher realms of thought. You will determine your own spiritual outlook by reaching the peak of your soul level. In your search for meaningful answers you will be confronted with your own fears, which will help you destroy any conventional or self-made ties holding you to material things or desires. You will strengthen that which is vitally important to your spiritual progress. Chains and restrictions will be broken, making way for ideas and goals which have long been waiting to take seed deep within you. You can easily abandon your false sense of security and find that the comforts you pursued were in fact blocking your spiritual journey. Embedded in man's mind are the safe, well-padded fears of his ancestors. To be man is to be free of anything that is not of his own belief; this can be determined by investigating the birth of any concept he holds dear. This is not to say that what you believe is meant to be destroyed, but rather that you should develop within yourself the original mold of your soul personality. The Hierophant becomes the spring cleaner, making way for summer glory and autumn acceptance. Winter then becomes the womb of eternity for further growth. The Hierophant can open the gate for you to "know thyself."

TIME:

The spiritual therapy of this meditation is truly effective for the student who is willing to gaze into the mirror of life and see himself as he really is. Total inner balance gives a wider view of the Divine Plan. If this meditation exercise is to be continuous, select the same time cycle each day until the meditation has been completed to your satisfaction.

HE:

SEPHIROTH = Triad of Intelligence
PATH = 16—Chesed—Chochma
HEBREW = Vau
ENGLISH = Nail

6 THE LOVERS

KEY:
Two paths, the time for choice, the outcome of which is of vital importance.

MEMORY:
Select well with integrity high;
Your moral scruples tell you why.

GUIDELINES:
Resist the temptation to change; stick to your resolutions, make firm decisions.

Is this situation what you really want?

Seek spiritual values; control your emotions and select your path with care.

REVERSE KEY:
Wanting the best of both worlds, causing everyone concerned to feel unstable.

MEMORY:
Indecision is not your friend;
You may lose all in the end.

GUIDELINES:
Temptation can be strong; be sure to make the right move.

Could indicate a severe break in a relationship. Quarrels, disagreement, separation or divorce.

Strong opposition is felt and the pressure can cause great concern.

COMPARISON CHART:
YOD:
TETRAGRAMMATON = VAU
PRINCIPLE = Triality
EXPRESSION = Spirit/Transformer/Universe/Material/Neutral

HE:
ASTROLOGY = Venus
GNOTHOLOGY = Harmony

6 THE LOVERS

VAU:
MEDITATION:

There is much depth in this meditation. The symbolic message of the Lovers can penetrate the ego and release the Karmic desire of the higher self. This intriguing symbol brings to your immediate attention that both man and woman are equally important in the divine scheme. They are represented here naked, stripped of their facade of ego. Behind the man is the Tree of Life, bearing 12 luscious fruits; behind the woman is the Tree of Knowledge, representing good and evil. Notice the serpent entwined around it. The initial interpretation conveys all that is human in the ways of love, the mysteries of male and female relationships which embrace innocence, romance, courtship and marriage. These include all the complications that lack of understanding between man and woman create. Going deeper into this beautiful symbol, we can see the young man looking up at the woman, but she does not return his look. The woman is looking at the angel Raphael, who is the angel of Air. Raphael continually bestows blessings upon humanity. Our lesson here is that man continually cuts himself off from blessings and guidance by using only his conscious intellect. Man represents the conscious intellect; by looking at the female, he is appealing to his subconscious, who in turn holds her head high and obtains divine wisdom and guidance from the superconscious, represented by Raphael. This uplifting meditation enables you to realize that when you feel alone it is only because you refuse to reach out for heavenly inspiration, the promise of the Almighty.

TIME:

Allow ample time for this deep meditation. Reflect on the ancient symbology which will lead you into higher paths of self-understanding via the conscious, subconscious and superconscious. The only resistance you will encounter is the conscious self, which is always on guard with reason and logic.

HE:
SEPHIROTH = Triad of Intelligence
PATH = 17 — Tiphares — Binah
HEBREW = Zain
ENGLISH = Sword

7 THE CHARIOT

KEY:
Important to exercise self-discipline. With continued effort you can win the day and be triumphant.

MEMORY:
Achievement now with
effort from you;
Control emotions,
dreams come true.

GUIDELINES:
Remove all obstacles and then you will have the vision to go ahead.

Honor, award or recognition is due to the client.

Harness your energy; it must be applied wisely or you will not make your point.

REVERSE KEY:
A portentous situation, indicating wrong use of energies and talent. Possible negative vibrations of unfairness, pressure, force.

MEMORY:
All is not well, this you
can see;
Living this way just cannot be.

GUIDELINES:
A Court Card within the spread indicates someone in your life who has no consideration or concern.

Wastefulness and indulgence can be your downfall.

Too much energy channelled through an overbearing attitude, and considerable application of unnecessary force.

7 THE CHARIOT

COMPARISON CHART:

YOD:

TETRAGRAMMATON = HE = YOD

PRINCIPLE = Substantiality

EXPRESSION = Father/Creator/God/Intellectual/Active

HE:

ASTROLOGY = Sagittarius

GNOTHOLOGY = Wisdom, —Inner Self

VAU:

MEDITATION:

As this beautiful meditation unfolds, one quickly senses the merging of divine forces which create a completely new vista of cosmic consciousness, revealing the unique necessity of positive and negative energies. The spiritual seeker learns that the portrayal of the princely being within the symbol is akin to the human body, which houses the spiritual forces of the soul. This majestic figure is like Apollo, who was the patron of light, life and healing. He represented the discipline and morals of human existence and the rules contained within the law of things. From Apollo and his followers we received the inspiring philosophy of *Gnothi Seauton* — Know Thyself. As we pursue our journey in this life we must be ever thoughtful of the flow of cosmic energies and the natural laws and be mindful of our ultimate goal, which should come to full realization by our controlling and understanding the God power within us all. We are indeed well blessed: the heavenly will is the gift of free will to all men. It is our divine inheritance to explore and realize the purpose of our existence and control our every act with the heavenly tools that God gave us.

TIME:

Understanding that life is affected by inner control, this meditation should be a priority for the student seeking order within himself. For the beginner I recommend regular meditation on this symbol to prepare for the balance needed for deeper comprehension. Three in the afternoon or three in the morning is the time cycle recommended to meditate on the symbol of the Chariot.

HE:

SEPHIROTH = Triad of Intelligence

PATH = 18 — Gevurah — Binah

HEBREW = Cheth

ENGLISH = Fence

8 STRENGTH

KEY:
The inner qualities representing love, patience and gentleness are superior to material power, force or hate.

MEMORY:
Use the love you feel
within;
Feed them honey and
you will win.

GUIDELINES:
A reconciliation is possible if you can conquer your emotions.

Take another look at the obstacles and see if they are real.

Success demands organization; then you will realize satisfaction and joy.

REVERSE KEY:
Do not lose your nerve or surrender; this will force you to resort to alternatives that can upset future plans.

MEMORY:
Heed the wisdom in this
card;
Issues forced make life
hard.

GUIDELINES:
A domineering attitude will not solve the problem; you must have harmony to succeed.

If you really believe that you are right, be firm but don't cause distress to others.

Reality must be faced; this will clarify the disturbing influences. You cannot progress unless you understand this fully.

8 STRENGTH

COMPARISON CHART:

YOD:

TETRAGRAMMATON = HE
PRINCIPLE = Imponderability
EXPRESSION = Siva/Receiver/Man/Moral/Passive

HE:

ASTROLOGY = Neptune
GNOTHOLOGY = Executive Power & Ability

VAU:

MEDITATION:

Self-discovery is the spiritual adventure of this meditation. We must truly have the desire to overcome material and spiritual barriers. So often in life these barriers loom before us, subjecting the soul to all the pain and misery that go with indecision. The questions that arise when we attempt to discipline our daily lives absorb so much energy. When we try to reason things out on our own, we experience anguish from a lack of faith which disconnects our spiritual lifeline. Through the high order of this symbol we can attain the knowledge we need to balance our lives. We may be tempted to resort to emotional reasoning instead of offering the need before the throne of God. Many despondent souls say that the problems they face are too heavy and complicated to take to the Almighty, yet they are willing to struggle and carry the burdens on their own shoulders. Let this meditation be the soothing balm for all your worries and problems; think how much easier life will be if you release your load to God. Then you will have the spiritual vision to greet each new day with total trust. Faith makes us strong; we become vulnerable when we allow others to take advantage of us, and in the struggle to protect ourselves we can easily become aggressive and evasive, casting a shadow on our relationship with the Almighty.

TIME:

Lighten your burden today and let your face feel the warmth of God's radiant light. The time for this meditation is whenever you are in need.

HE:

SEPHIROTH = Triad of Morality
PATH = 19 — Gevurah — Chesed
HEBREW = Teth
ENGLISH = Serpent

9 THE HERMIT

KEY:
Ask and it shall be given you; seek, and ye shall find; knock and it shall be opened to you. The promise of Christ can be found in your own heart.

MEMORY:
Look up, dear friend,
and see the light;
It shines by day and
shines by night.

GUIDELINES:
Guidance and help are available, but the ultimate responsibility is yours.

There is an answer and you have the ability to solve the situation.

Experiment, but take it easy. Use discretion until you are completely sure.

REVERSE KEY:
Too much resistance, objection. A refusal to accept or listen to good counsel. Don't let ego stand between you and good sense.

MEMORY:
Swallow pride, why
don't you ask?
Halve the problem, half
the task.

GUIDELINES:
Need to stop present activity, take time to plan carefully before going ahead.

Lack of communication. Trying to cut yourself off from others.

A feeling of isolation, no one seems to care. Change your attitude and things will look better.

9 THE HERMIT

COMPARISON CHART:

YOD:
TETRAGRAMMATON = VAU
PRINCIPLE: = Triality
EXPRESSION = Spirit/Transformer/Universe/Material/Neutral

HE:
ASTROLOGY = Aquarius
GNOTHOLOGY = Universalism

VAU:
MEDITATION:

This meditation will bring the heavenly fruits of wisdom offered by the Hermit on the peak. To reach this peak you must leave wordly cares behind and strive to reach the top. By constant spiritual effort, you will be encouraged to leave the security of your ego and forget the importance of earthly endeavor. In turn, you will receive the ability to radiate a higher force and help light the way for others. This spiritual climb will not make you a recluse but rather a lantern for fellow souls in distress. Soon you will sense the peaceful vibrations that give comfort when the need arises. They will fortify you during your daily activities, and others will be drawn towards you without knowing why, feeling refreshed from the vibrations around you. Look up even now and see His light, feel the rays of self-acceptance and self-confidence permeate your whole being. This inspiring meditation is comparable to billions of health-giving light rays, and your blessings will be so numerous that all those around you will also receive benefits.

TIME:

Greet the first light with this inspiring devotion and then go on your way and let others feel the wonder of Christ in you.

HE:
SEPHIROTH = Triad of Morality
PATH = 20—Tiphares—Chesed
HEBREW = Yod
ENGLISH = Hand

10 WHEEL OF FORTUNE

KEY:
Remember, when you are down on the Wheel of Life there is only one way to go: up.

MEMORY:
The Wheel of Life spins
round for man,
You must adapt the best
you can.

GUIDELINES:
Do not begin to feel sorry for yourself. Look for new opportunities.

Change could be exactly what you need at this time. Examine new ideas carefully before discarding them.

Exercise your own strength; be prepared to adapt to different circumstances.

REVERSE KEY:
Everything may appear to be wrong no matter how hard you try. Have courage, be strong, put your thoughts on higher things.

MEMORY:
When you can't see the
way to go,
Trust in God and let Him
know.

GUIDELINES:
Being irritable or depressed can only make your situation worse.

Perhaps you put too high a price on your own ego. Take stock and reevaluate your abilities.

Analyze everything carefully: will you benefit by this experience?

10 WHEEL OF FORTUNE

COMPARISON CHART:

YOD:
TETRAGRAMMATON = HE = YOD
PRINCIPLE = Substantiality
EXPRESSION = Father/Creator/God/Intellectual/Active

HE:
ASTROLOGY = Uranus
GNOTHOLOGY = Master Number 11

VAU:

MEDITATION:

Understanding the rhythm of life can mean the unfolding of nature's secrets. Take the time to look back, try to re-experience past happiness and sorrows, see what you considered important in your life at that time. Examine the results of the efforts you made and what you had to do to attain or lose things that you held dear. See how your needs have changed as the Wheel of Life has turned, see how nature falls beautifully into a nonresisting pattern, greeting spring but not demanding the fruits of harvest. Nature accepts the pattern of things, and each part of the yearly cycle is for a definite purpose. Consequently, we have the continuous pattern and rhythm of the seasons. Is your life flowing peacefully, do you accept that which is inevitable? Or do you work against life? Attune yourself to the rhythm of life, know that there is a time to plant, a time to wait and a time to reap the harvest. Try to understand that if you do not plant a seed then you cannot expect a harvest. If you find that you continually make the same mistakes, try to look back and understand why. Realize that every new day brings new opportunities and new challenges. Develop patience; if you have done the right things, then the right things will happen. Be still awhile and allow your body and mind to tune in to the rhythm of the universe. Come to God as a child, let him know all your mistakes, and trust in Him. Have no fears, let your tomorrows rest with God.

TIME:

Never go to sleep depressed; take a good look at the Wheel of Life and know that you are protected. Learn to accept the ups and downs, and meditate on this symbol before retiring.

HE:
SEPHIROTH = Triad of Morality
PATH = 21—Netzach—Chesed
HEBREW = Kaph
ENGLISH = Palm of the Hand

11 JUSTICE

KEY:
Someone has investigated the situation concerned and has arrived at a decision that is fair and honest.

MEMORY:
Justice given, lesson learned;
We receive what we have earned.

GUIDELINES:
Stick to your guns, don't be influenced by persuasive talk.

You should have learned by past experience to do what you feel is best.

All things being considered, the right decision has been made.

REVERSE KEY:
Injustice and possible loss. Someone feels inadequate and is unable to change the situation.

MEMORY:
No matter what is right or true,
You cannot change what people do.

GUIDELINES:
Someone has taken advantage of you, and at this time you cannot change things.

You have done everything possible; stop worrying and direct your energies elsewhere.

A Karmic lesson that must be fully understood. Accept it and go your way.

11 JUSTICE

COMPARISON CHART:

YOD:
TETRAGRAMMATON = HE
PRINCIPLE = Imponderability
EXPRESSION = Son/Receiver/
Man/Moral/
Passive

HE:
ASTROLOGY = Capricorn
GNOTHOLOGY = Individuality

VAU:

MEDITATION:

To become involved with the Higher Self is to know your purpose here on earth. You were not meant to be a prisoner in your earthly body; once you understand that you are a soul with a body and have access to the higher realms of consciousness, you can overcome the restrictions of earthly thoughts. You must learn to judge yourself and analyze your actions. Often we are inundated with higher thoughts and resort to the negative barriers we create in our conscious mind. Careless application of our thoughts shows in our actions, which disappoints those we love and offends our higher consciousness. Total balance is needed; to achieve this we must learn to understand the power we have over our own existence. How can we have high, noble thoughts and then commit deeds that make us ashamed? Once we learn to blend the Higher Self with our daily thinking pattern, we will learn how to avoid the pitfalls experienced when we operate only on a materialistic level. As we learn to blend the two levels, we will blossom and mature spiritually. We will grow stronger and develop an inner strength that will help us to steer our lives in the right direction. Perfect balance within gives great strength to character, and in this strength is a beautiful peace that passeth all understanding.

TIME:

Reaching total balance takes time to eliminate all negative thought vibrations. Choose a time when you can concentrate and relax completely. This is a beautiful outdoor meditation; nature can help you regain your equilibrium if you choose a quiet spot in the forest, by a stream or up in the mountains.

HE:
SEPHIROTH = Triad of Morality
PATH = 22—Tiphares—Gevurah
HEBREW = Lamed
ENGLISH = Ox-goad

12 THE HANGED MAN

KEY:
Piercing the barrier of limited consciousness and availing yourself of higher wisdom.

MEMORY:
Blessed with truth and has no fear;
Faith holds strong when trouble's near.

GUIDELINES:
Able to look above present situation and conditions. You have great foresight and stamina.

Don't be misled, there is plenty of action behind the apparent standstill. Be prepared for new and innovative ideas. Could be a complete and unexpected change at home or at work.

The pussycat is now ready to roar like a lion. Unexpected views, attitudes or decisions on the horizon.

REVERSE KEY:
Content with present environment and circumstances. Apt to be preoccupied with material matters.

MEMORY:
Absorbed in earthly work and gain;
Oblivious to your spiritual pain.

GUIDELINES:
Watch out for a do-gooder or someone with many promises; consider carefully before becoming involved.

Time to get out from under. You're surrounded by false securities. You need to recognize your own ability and build with your own plans.

Outward appearances don't necessarily present the true picture. Hold something in reserve.

12 THE HANGED MAN

COMPARISON CHART:

YOD:
TETRAGRAMMATON = VAU
PRINCIPLE = Triality
EXPRESSION = Spirit/Transformer/Universe/Material/Neutral

HE:
ASTROLOGY = Pisces
GNOTHOLOGY = Cooperation

VAU:

MEDITATION:

Only when you are ready to submit to the higher vibratory forces can you be released from the turmoil resulting from your own actions. Meditation is the first step toward this goal. Begin by asking the God force to release you from all your fears, to silence your racing thoughts and help you to prepare for the peace that passeth all understanding. Learn to relax both physically and mentally, allow the higher forces to renew your existence. Be tolerant of all things and know that you are an essential part of the life force around you. Ask the almighty forces to uplift your soul and open your eyes to spiritual vision so that you may see and understand your purpose here on earth. All of us have a purpose, we were not meant to go on from day to day concerned only with material matters. Within us is the God essence that is waiting to merge with the universal forces. Only when we are totally willing to hear the word of God will it be spoken to us. In this beautiful meditation leave all wordly concerns behind and step into the higher vibrations, so that you may know the path that has been chosen for your earthly experience.

TIME:

The early hours of the morning, when the thought vibrations of others are asleep, is an ideal time to reach out to the God force and learn your purpose in life.

HE:
SEPHIROTH = Triad of Morality
PATH = 23—Hod—Gevurah
HEBREW = Mem
ENGLISH = Water

13 DEATH (Transition)

KEY:
Do not resist sudden change; the vibratory force around you will provide all the strength needed to accept new situations.

MEMORY:
Release your fears and look ahead;
Today is new, the past is dead.

GUIDELINES:
You must try and leave the past behind you; if you hang on you will lose new opportunities coming into your life.

Experience is the greatest teacher; don't be afraid to start new projects.

Worry and depression will get you nowhere. Face the future with new faith and accept the changes.

REVERSE KEY:
A feeling of limbo or perhaps depression. In need of new ideas and motivation. Success after a time and reorganization. Depending on format of spread, could indicate a birth.

MEMORY:
Time and work will change it all;
Stand up straight or you may fall.

GUIDELINES:
Come to grips with life, don't let things slide. Nothing will happen unless you make it happen.

If affairs appear to be at a standstill, keep your mind active and plan ahead for the future.

Your hands may be tied but not your mind. Make new goals and plan carefully. Wait for the right time to pursue them.

13 DEATH

COMPARISON CHART:

YOD:
TETRAGRAMMATON = HE = YOD
PRINCIPLE = Substantiality
EXPRESSION = Father/Creator/God/Intellecual/Active

HE:
ASTROLOGY = Aries
GNOTHOLOGY = Self-expression

VAU:

MEDITATION:

Renewed life energies await the soul who is willing to release itself from the bondage and limitations of this earth. You must learn to understand that Death is non-existent. This beautiful symbol of the Major Arcana helps to unfold the mysteries of transition. Death as we fear it does not exist; life is continually changing from one level of consciousness to another. Look back on your life and consider the many changes you have experienced. When something was apparently taken away, time will show you the natural rhythmic pattern and you will see that something important was put in its place. Think about nature and all her seasons, pause for a moment and focus your mind on the wonders of the universe. See yourself as an integral part of this magnificent plan. Try to understand your purpose here on earth. Contemplate the life of Christ, walk with Him and hear His message. Help him to carry His cross and meditate on the resurrection. Ask God in His mercy to relieve you of all your fears and fill your heart with His glorious faith. Ask to be born again, make new plans and enjoy each new day that is given to you. Fill your life with new hope, leave all your yesterdays behind and feel the joy of the Living God born again within you.

TIME:

Wherever you may be and at whatever time you desire to experience rebirth of the Spirit, meditate on the symbol of Transition.

HE:
SEPHIROTH = Triad of Morality
PATH = 24—Netzach—Tiphares
HEBREW = Nun
ENGLISH = Fish

14 TEMPERANCE

KEY:
Try new things, but keep a hold on your present security. At this time it is important to maintain a balance in your life.

MEMORY:
Patience builds the dreams of man;
Maintain balance while you plan.

GUIDELINES:
Easy does it, don't rush anything at this time. Keep your cool.

Don't give up your security; you need more time before making any major decisions.

Don't overdo things; take life at a moderate pace. Patience will win in the end.

REVERSE KEY:
A great need to stop and consider how things are going in your life. Good ideas need a well-planned program before going ahead. Energies are being wasted and scattered.

MEMORY:
Too much too soon can ruin it all;
Without foundations you will fall.

GUIDELINES:
Emotional stress caused through frustration. Judgment is lacking; look before you leap.

Slow down and re-evaluate everything. Continual pushing will not put things in order. A different approach is required.

Conflict in personal and business affairs. Forcing the issue is not the answer. There's a need for total change.

14 TEMPERANCE

COMPARISON CHART:

YOD:
TETRAGRAMMATON = HE
PRINCIPLE = Imponderability
EXPRESSION = Son/Receiver/ Man/Moral/Passive

HE:
ASTROLOGY = Taurus
GNOTHOLOGY = Self-discipline

VAU:

MEDITATION:

The symbol of Temperance is the key to higher planes of consciousness, releasing the ego and aspiring to the spiritual vision of the Higher Self. Man is a soul with a physical body and he must endeavor to look beyond the limitations he creates for himself. Rising to a higher level can result in many changes and bring about the rapid development of the psychic senses. When man learns to balance his earthly life he is in touch with his higher consciousness. As man is an essential part of the universal plan, he has stored within him the secrets of the universe. To unlock the door he must be prepared to live a spiritual life here on earth but be concerned with both material and spiritual matters, creating for himself tranquility, balance and harmony. It is in this state of perfect equilibrium that he will discover his true purpose here on earth. His vision will be extended beyond this world, he will be blessed with knowledge from the higher planes and his path will be made clear. To achieve this union with the Higher Self, we must leave behind our earthly desires and adjust our lives to absorb the lesson of this symbol.

TIME:

In the morning before noon, preferably in the open air, taking time to relax and become in tune with the universe.

HE:
SEPHIROTH = Triad of Morality
PATH = 25—Yesod—Tiphares
HEBREW = Samech
ENGLISH = Prop

15 THE DEVIL

KEY:
Too involved and wrapped up in material concerns. Your journey in life is off course and you are now traveling up a dead-end street.

MEMORY:
Chains you grasped to
change your life
Now hold you tight and
cause you strife.

GUIDELINES:
Indulgence has created a miserable existence. Recognize what is happening around you and make amends.

A feeling of pressure and force brought about by lack of consideration and selfishness.

Bogged down with a sense of hopelessness, by your own efforts you can start again.

REVERSE KEY:
Indecision is weakness and can cause instability. Now that you have seen the light, you should resond quickly and free yourself from past habits.

MEMORY:
Listen to your higher
voice;
Chance your ways, you
have the choice.

GUIDELINES:
You have been influenced, and now that you recognize this fact, it is time to take the necessary action against this influence.

It's never too late to make amends; deal with your problems and avoid emotional outbreaks.

Being timid will only emphasize your weakness. Take the bull by the horns and do your own thing.

15 THE DEVIL

COMPARISON CHART:

YOD:
TETRAGRAMMATON = VAU
PRINCIPLE = Triality
EXPRESSION = Spirit/Transformer/Universe/Material/Neutral

HE:
ASTROLOGY = Saturn
GNOTHOLOGY = Freedom

VAU:

MEDITATION:

When one feels completely submerged in material matters, the soul appeals to the mind, longing for inner peace. The inner voice should not be ignored, you must learn to respond to your spiritual needs in the same way that you seek medical help when your body feels pain. If your life is in a turmoil, meditation on this symbol will help you contact your real needs. Ambition and progress should not be confused with greed and selfishness. As you enter into meditation, examine your goals, look at the people around you and see how they are affected by your needs. Are you tied to earthly concerns and physical desires? Do you find room in your prayers to pray for others as well as your own requirements? Ask your heavenly Father to help you on your earthly journey but not at the expense of others. Come as a little child and ask for the self-made chains to be broken, leaving you free to make amends. As you lift your thoughts and prayers to a higher plane of consciousness, be truly sorry for any hurt you may have caused others and ask God to show you how to use your earthly energies for the good of those around you. Drink in His mercy, thank Him for His goodness and may the energies you feel be transformed into pure light for others to see.

TIME:

Before retiring, bathe and wear a loose robe. Sit on the floor cross-legged or in a straight-backed chair. Meditate on this symbol until you feel the forgiveness of your Higher Self flowing into your conscious thoughts.

HE:
SEPHIROTH = Triad of Materialism
PATH = 26 — Hod — Tiphares
HEBREW = Ayin
ENGLISH = Eye

16 THE TOWER

KEY:
Take a good long look at your life. Situation will change rapidly; be prepared.

MEMORY:
This Karmic force will clear away
The debris caused by yesterday.

GUIDELINES:
Change is inevitable; Karmic forces will cause a breakdown in relationship, business, finances or any situation you consider permanent.

Release the old way of life. Rather than lament the past, accept the changes and plan for the future.

Clinging to old goals will prevent you from accepting new and wonderful opportunities in the future.

REVERSE KEY:
The process of change has started; don't try to resist the inevitable breakdown of present circumstances.

MEMORY:
The time has come to see the light;
Let it go, don't try to fight.

GUIDELINES:
Look at things as they really are. Don't be put off by false ideas. Ignore any opposition and you will win the day.

See the writing on the wall and do what you know is right. Don't wait till the last minute.

Trying to hang on will only make the situation worse. Clear things up and have the courage to start over.

16 THE TOWER

COMPARISON CHART:

YOD:

TETRAGRAMMATON = HE = YOD

PRINCIPLE = Substantiality

EXPRESSION = Father/Creator/God/Intellectual/Active

HE:

ASTROLOGY = Mars

GNOTHOLOGY = Harmony

VAU:

MEDITATION:

Loneliness can lead you to meditate on this beautiful symbol. No matter how well we build forces within, the universe can destroy our hopes and dreams. To know God we must realize the false securities we have built around us and how easily they can disappear. Seek a greater strength, the strength of your Father in Heaven. Reach out for the protection of the heavenly forces and feel the everlasting love of God fill you anew with courage to overcome any difficulty you may encounter. Take a good look at your life and pray for the mercy of God to take away all that has been built falsely. Don't be afraid to see yourself as you really are, for you are a child of God and in recognizing your true self you will be blessed with peace and happiness. If you feel lost on the path of life, have faith and in this meditation feel the loving strength of your heavenly Father in every fiber of your being. Do not live in fear; He loves you as no other can. In the darkness of despair, believe in the radiant light of Christ and your soul will be filled with His glory.

TIME:

At three o'clock in the afternoon you will feel more attuned to the power of this meditation. Allow sufficient time for the vibrations to give you all the strength you need.

HE:

SEPHIROTH = Triad of Materialism

PATH = 27—Hod—Netzach

HEBREW = Peh

ENGLISH = Mouth

17 THE STAR

KEY:
This beautiful symbol indicates the future accomplishment of goals presently being developed.

MEMORY:
Inspiration, hope and health,
Spiritual gifts beyond one's self.

GUIDELINES:
You are well blessed and can expect much spiritual help and guidance in all endeavors.

On the right path, foundations are good. Keep your eyes on the Star and you will achieve your goals.

Health situation will improve; strong spiritual forces surround you.

REVERSE KEY:
Through lack of judgment, loss will be incurred. Could indicate ill health.

MEMORY:
From wrong path, loss may occur;
Sickness may your vision blur.

GUIDELINES:
A pessimistic attitude will narrow your relationships and cut off any possibility of renewal.

In this present condition it would be wise to contemplate past mistakes and put things into perspective.

A sense of hopelessness but all is not lost. Illness is indicated, depending on your question and on cards in the spread.

17 THE STAR

COMPARISON CHART:

YOD:
TETRAGRAMMATON = HE
PRINCIPLE = Imponderability
EXPRESSION = Son/Receiver/ Man/Moral/ Passive

HE:
ASTROLOGY = Gemini
GNOTHOLOGY = Inner Wisdom

VAU:

MEDITATION:

Trying to comprehend the universal consciousness, we must recognize that it is far beyond our own understanding. We cannot possibly comprehend the intellect of the Superconscious with our earthly minds. Consequently, we must learn to pierce the darkness by submitting ourselves completely to the God force. We must go to the source without question, for we could not understand the answer. By submitting our spirits to the Heavenly Spirit, we will lose our petty desires and earthly concerns. The first part of our heavenly journey will make us aware of our own individuality, and by concentrating on the pure essence of life, we will merge slowly and beautifully with the God force. As this miracle of true belonging takes place, we will become stronger and stronger — the universal forces will absorb every atom of our being. In this journey of consciousness, we will touch the mercy of God and experience for a short time the true meaning of LOVE. As we progress, we will also know the true meaning of pain. In all our meditations using the Star as our spiritual focus, we will arrive back at earthly consciousness more aware and thankful for the many blessings that have been given to us.

TIME:

Allow extra time for this absorbing meditation. Time is needed to rid ourselves of earthly concerns before reaching out to the universal forces. After the meditation take time to contemplate and write down your experience with the Star.

HE:
SEPHIROTH = Triad of Materialism
PATH = 15—Tiphares—Chochma
HEBREW = Heh
ENGLISH = Window

18 THE MOON

KEY:
Be alert for any subtle changes; don't be deceived by apparent security. Allow your intuitive powers to guide you.

MEMORY:
Deep inside you will know
Change has come, though it won't show.

GUIDELINES:
Make notes of any dreams or intuitive feelings. Could indicate the beginning of psychic development.

Learn to be more independent and trust your own feelings. Build your own security and do not lean too much on others.

If you have concerns relating to others, clear the air and let them know where you stand.

REVERSE KEY:
Don't take any risks at this time. Possibility of misunderstanding; don't make changes, wait till the storm is over.

MEMORY:
Make no judgement at this date;
Things will clear up if you wait.

GUIDELINES:
Don't waste energies in arguments or disagreements. Hold on to your point of view and add a dash of patience.

Don't be afraid to see things as they really are. Be in complete control of your own emotions.

Don't let your imagination run away with you. Keep control and the situation will right itself in your favor.

18 THE MOON

COMPARISON CHART:

YOD:
TETRAGRAMMATON = VAU
PRINCIPLE = Triality
EXPRESSION = Spirit/Transformer/Universe/Material/Neutral

HE:
ASTROLOGY = Cancer
GNOTHOLOGY = Power & Ability

VAU:

MEDITATION:

Faith is our greatest friend. Our faith is often tested; not always by others but by ourselves. When we lack faith we experience being totally alone. Faith is the shadow of our higher self that remains here on earth to remind us of our purpose in the universe. Faith is a reflection of what our higher consciusness knows to be true. Our very existence is a living faith of the Living Christ. Without faith we are vulnerable and can easily succumb to failure, for there is nothing to support our ideals and goals in life. When pressure is released, our inner being is capable of seeing future possibilities. It is only when we allow earthly concerns to fill our minds that we lose sight of lofty goals. We are part of this glorious creation and divided from our higher consciousness by lack of faith. Help us, dear Lord, to strengthen our faith so that we may understand the greatness You have bestowed upon us. Fill our lives with divine healing rays that penetrate our conscious thoughts, so that we may consciously build our faith in the blessings You give us daily.

TIME:

Upon going to bed prepare for this uplifting meditation and ask the Divine Consciousness to fill you with everlasting faith. Wake up in the morning and know that you have been blessed and let faith be your constant companion.

HE:
SEPHIROTH = Triad of Materialism
PATH = 29—Malcuth—Netzach
HEBREW = Qoph
ENGLISH = Back of the Head

19 THE SUN

KEY:
Regardless of present circumstances, when this vibrant symbol is the outcome of the spread, There will be joy and happiness in your future.

MEMORY:
Attainment, joy and happiness?
With Sun in spread, the answer's yes.

GUIDELINES:
Opportunity is in the offing. Take it with both hands. Don't hesitate to go ahead.

Many blessings; a time to be happy and give thanks.

Success lies ahead and growth of personal wealth. New ventures will prosper. Good health will be yours.

REVERSE KEY:
Need for a realistic outlook on life. Be perfectly honest with yourself. Stop day-dreaming and put some effort into reaching your goals. Depression or failure is not for you.

MEMORY:
A sense of failure, loss involved;
Apply yourself till problem's solved.

GUIDELINES:
Before becoming involved in any project, investigate all aspects first. Don't let anyone pull the wool over your eyes.

Disagreements and misunderstandings can affect close relationships. Future plans may have to be canceled.

Disappointment at home or at work. Loss can be associated with this reverse symbol.

19 THE SUN

COMPARISON CHART:

YOD:

TETRAGRAMMATON = HE = YOD
PRINCIPLE = Substantiality
EXPRESSION = Father/Creator/God/Intellectual/Active

HE:

ASTROLOGY = Leo
GNOTHOLOGY = Humanitarian

VAU:

MEDITATION:

Liberate me, Lord, from selfishness and fear. Fill my soul with Thy heavenly radiance. Open my eyes so that I may see the many blessings Thou hast given. As I sleep may my soul rejoice and sing Thy praises in the company of angels. When all is dark around me let the universal light fill me with Thy everlasting glory. Free me from selfish desires so that I may help others to know Thee. In the magnificant design of the universe Thou hast granted me a place. I may not have any importance here on earth but I am an important part of Thy holy plan. Help me to recognize my purpose here on earth and to be thankful for all that has been given to me. This day, dear Lord, walk with me, let me hear Thy voice in the demands of others; let me feel Thy touch in the tools I work with. Let me see Thy splendor in the eyes of everyone I meet. Feel my need and hear my prayer, and when this day comes to a close, may the deeds I have done be acceptable to Thee. In Thy love I am protected; help me to love others and make no demands. Fill my mind and body with Thy living light, take away my constant fears and teach me to focus my life on Jesus Christ. This day may He walk with me and give me the strength to overcome all my weaknesses. I ask that each thought be purified by His divine presence and that His glory light my way.

TIME:

Before commencing the day's activities, meditate on the magnificent symbol of the Sun. Share this light with all you meet and let it radiate into any dark places you may encounter.

HE:

SEPHIROTH = Triad of Materialism
PATH = 30 — Yesod — Hod
HEBREW = Resh
ENGLISH = Head

20 JUDGEMENT

KEY:
Wonderful things are starting to happen. You have the ability to forge ahead and see what the future holds. Break away from conventional thinking and face life realistically.

MEMORY:
New vibrations let you
see
Exactly what you'd like
to be.

GUIDELINES:
By taking a good look at your life you will be gifted with the vision to see ahead.

So far, so good. You are being blessed with cosmic energies that will give you the guidance you need.

No need for any unwanted ties; now is the time to direct yourself and make all the changes you desire.

REVERSE KEY:
Uneasy feeling, lonely and often in a self-made rut. Longing to be free of certain situations but cannot see a way out.

MEMORY:
This soul is tired and
feeling low;
Would like to know
which way to go.

GUIDELINES:
Feeling sorry for yourself will not help the situation. Time to review your life to date and make plans for the future.

Release yourself, don't allow fear to keep you locked into a situation. Try new ideas, a new job, or maybe move far away and start again.

Loneliness or sickness can be affecting you. Consider the spread carefully and you will be able to find help.

20 JUDGEMENT

COMPARISON CHART:

YOD:
TETRAGRAMMATON = HE
PRINCIPLE = Imponderability
EXPRESSION = Son/Receiver/Man/Moral/Passive

HE:
ASTROLOGY = Moon
GNOTHOLOGY = Master Number 22

VAU:
MEDITATION:

Why am I here, dear Father? What is my purpose? Help me to rise above my daily thinking and reach the heavenly consciousness within me. Open the doors of my higher consciousness so that I may see my purpose here on earth. What souls must I touch with kindness? Who have I ignored in my daily task of pleasing myself? Let me accomplish my spiritual mission, place before me all the things I have done and all the things I have not done. Give me the courage to look at myself and recognize what is lacking. Open my eyes, dear Father, and let me see my miserable existence. By simple prayer let my soul be born again and see the work I have to accomplish. May the heavenly forces guide me to those in need, and in Thy mercy allow me to begin new and worthwhile spiritual growth. As my body sleeps and prepares for the following day, let my consciousness rise to the heavenly spheres and receive the gift of love, so that I may be strong in all I have to do. Help me to forgive myself and to accept Thy everlasting mercy.

TIME:

A quiet period before going to bed. Contemplate the earthly mission of your soul and request conscious knowledge of your purpose in this life.

HE:
SEPHIROTH = Triad of Materialism
PATH = 31 — Malcuth — Hod
HEBREW = Shin
ENGLISH = Tooth

21 THE WORLD

KEY:
Now you're free to go in any direction; a job well done. You will be triumphant in any undertaking.

MEMORY:
Free to choose your path
at last;
You've learned your lessons in the past.

GUIDELINES:
Vibrations are good for any changes concerning home or job. You are free to accept new responsibilities; you can make others happy too.

Having insight, you have applied yourself well. It is within your power to make important decisions; others will rely on you.

Never forget what it took to get here. Your consciousness is now ready to reach a higher level.

REVERSE KEY:
A refusal to explore new horizons. Because of your reluctance to try new ideas, fear will create stagnation.

MEMORY:
Afraid of change and insecure;
Lack of vision will keep
you poor.

GUIDELINES:
You have experienced many lessons in life but are unable to learn from them. You are inclined to resist change and appear to enjoy being in a rut.

You're trying very hard but not applying yourself in the right way. You need encouragement to try new and different things.

A stubborn attitude will not lend itself to success. You must be prepared to accept other people's ideas as well as your own.

21 THE WORLD

COMPARISON CHART:

YOD:
TETRAGRAMMATON = VAU
PRINCIPLE = Triality
EXPRESSION = Spirit/Transformer/Universe/Material/Neutral

HE:
ASTROLOGY = Sun
GNOTHOLOGY = Master Number 33

VAU:
MEDITATION:

Although my soul is rich with the experience of many lifetimes, each day is a challenge, for my life is continually changing. I know it is Thy will that I exist; I also know that it is my fault when my life is out of balance. Help me on the sea of life to overcome the constant storms. When I am lonely and afraid, let me hear Thy voice in the darkness. Thy will, dear Lord, not mine be done. Only let me feel the nearness of Christ and I know that I can face the many problems that come into my life. Teach me to let go and not cling to earthly security. I ask for Thy divine power to enter my body and soul, healing all the hurts that are harbored there. Help me to release myself from all false ideas and security. Put in my hand the staff of true light, so that I may see which way to direct my soul. Help me to accept constant changes and to know that as I experience each new day in Christ, I come nearer to the Savior of mankind.

TIME:

When the pressures of life seem to be overpowering, take the time to meditate on the World symbol and you will soon realize how insignificant your troubles are. A few moments with Christ can change your whole life.

HE:
SEPHIROTH = Triad of Materialism
PATH = 32—Yesod—Malcuth
HEBREW = Tau
ENGLISH = Tau or Cross

SECTION III

CHAPTER 10
STEPS TO DIVINATION

The purpose of this chapter is to provide you with a list of procedures necessary for you to understand and complete prior to spreading the cards for divination. If you have thoroughly absorbed the information in the preceding chapters and have practiced the exercises faithfully, you should be ready to commence reading the cards seriously—either for yourself or for another person.

I have arranged this information in the form of nine simple steps, which should make it easier for you to commit them to memory, so that they become second nature to you before each reading.

During the course of explaining these steps, I may repeat some of the material you have studied earlier. Bear with me—the repetition will do no harm and will serve to imprint even further in your subconscious information which will aid you during divination.

Here are the nine steps you should complete before beginning any divination:

1. Arrange for the proper atmosphere.
2. Assume the proper seating position.
3. Prepare the Tarot deck, table and cover.
4. Have the client write out the question.
5. Recite the Prayer of Invocation.
6. Break the pack.
7. Have the client perform the preliminary procedures.
8. Perform the Ritual of Solidification.
9. Commence the spread.

Arrange for the Proper Atmosphere

If possible, try to arrange a special area or corner somewhere in your home to be used for Tarot study and divination and nothing else. This place should be quiet and undisturbed by outside activities and distractions. Your Tarot table, cloth and cards should be kept here when not in use. Whenever possible, fresh flowers add a positive and relaxing note; it is good to have them on the table even when you are not using the cards.

Another pleasant aid to concentration and relaxation is incense. It should not be so strong as to be overpowering, but a light fragrance that lends a mood to the situation, making it different from the normal routine of home or work. If you use it consistently, your subconscious will learn to associate the fragrance with your desire to probe the Higher Consciousness, and the incense will thus become an extra tool to aid you in your spiritual endeavors. Incense has traditionally been used as a spiritual cleanser by religions all over the world for thousands of years.

Assume the Proper Seating Position

A person who has developed his inner awareness to a high level or is considered to be "intuitive" is similar to a battery that has been fully charged. Such a person can tune in to the higher vibrations at any time and at any place, absorbing cosmic energy, storing it and releasing it whenever necessary for his own benefit or the benefit of others. Such a "release" of energy occurs during a divination.

The magnetic and psychic energy currents of the earth are said to flow from North to South and back again. The esoteric "Seat of Authority" is considered to be in the North, so you should arrange the seating for yourself and your client to line up NORTH and SOUTH. You should be sitting on the NORTH SIDE of the Tarot table, FACING SOUTH; your client should be sitting on the SOUTH SIDE of the Tarot table, FACING NORTH. This arrangement will align you and the client in the most harmonious position with the earth currents.

However, it is important to note that if you are using the Tarot ALONE, you should sit FACING EAST, the direction of the rising sun. This was considered especially beneficial by ancient scholars, as facing the direction of "the most pure representation of the first emanation from God."

This esoteric law of magnetic alignment is not restricted to the practice of Tarot. It should be used for any kind of spiritual study or divination. You will also find that you achieve a deeper, more restful sleep if your bed is aligned North-South; try it and see. I believe you will find a definite change in your studies and consultations if you adhere to this rule of the esoteric compass.

Prepare the Tarot Deck, Table and Cover

A natural wooden table — or at least, one with a wooden top — about two feet square is ideal for divination and study. When not in use it should be covered with a "Tarot Cover," a piece of cloth about two feet square, preferably silk. Keeping the surface of your table covered will protect it from attracting other vibratory influences. Natural wood is a good conductor of psychic energy and draws it like a magnet. By constantly working on your table, you "season" it favorably to your own vibrations, just as you do with your Tarot deck.

So you and your client are now seated at the table, facing North-South. Your cards have been unwrapped from their protective cloth and laid on the table. You are almost ready to begin the reading, but first there are a few more steps to accomplish.

Have the Client Write Out the Question

Always have a small note pad and pencil available. The pad should be just large enough for the client to write a question on; three inches by five inches is a good size. Keep the pad exclusively for Tarot use and use a wooden pencil, which is much better than a ballpoint pen. Choose a color pencil that you associate with the Tarot, perhaps one that is the same as or harmonizes with the color of your Tarot Cover.

There is a very definite reason why it is desirable to have your client write out the question. The ordinary human mind finds it very difficult to hold only one thought for any length of time; one thought leads to another, and another, flitting from subject to subject, triggering a kind of mental chain reaction. This is one of the initial difficulties the student of occultism discovers when attempting meditation for the first time. Now all of this additional mental activity can be very disturbing and confusing to the reader's concentration and can cause negative vibrations to influence the Tarot cards. If the client's thoughts are not focused on one question, it is possible to have a reading which is incorrect but not untruthful. In other words, if the reader is misled by negative or conflicting thoughts in the client's mind, the reader may give the wrong answer to the question but still be right, based on the information psychically received from the client's wandering thoughts. So, to avoid the possibility of this kind of situation, always have the client write down his question *clearly* and *simply*. Then have the client tear off the page and place it before him. Ask him to concentrate *only* on what he has written while he is shuffling the cards.

Note that the above procedure applies *only* when the client has a specific question to ask. If there is no specific question, and you are satisfied from talking with him that he is not withholding a question of some sort, you may ask for general spiritual guidance for him by requesting the "Wisdom of the Tarot." When this is the case, it is the same as saying, "Thy will, not mine, be done." Preconceived ideas and the need to receive answers do not fit into this method of divination; asking for this type of guidance is an expression of spiritual need. You should do two things to prepare for a spiritual divination:

1. Ask the client to write "Wisdom of the Tarot" on the pad and place the sheet in front of him.
2. Extract the Minor Arcana from your deck and commence the reading using only the Major Arcana, as they directly pertain to spiritual matters.

The type of spread suitable for the "Wisdom of the Tarot" is limited because of its profound nature; in the next chapter we will study the different spreads in detail.

After the reading, you should destroy the paper with the question or the "Wisdom" request on it. This will reassure the client and also remove any existing vibrations left in the ether concerning the question.

Recite the Prayer of Invocation

Anyone who takes upon himself the responsibility of offering guidance on behalf of the Supreme Force first requires quidance for himself. As we open our minds and souls to the Higher Consciousness, we must be certain that our channel is clear and true, so that the wisdom we receive will likewise be true and provide the proper guidance for the client.

Contact with the Supreme Force should be made through prayer, just like a phone call. Prayer is like a lifeline — it feels good to have its security around you, to feel the warmth and comfort of Almighty Love as you undertake the serious responsibility of counselling others.

Before commencing the reading, therefore, I recommend that you recite the following prayer silently:

INVOCATION

Dear Heavenly Father, I entreat Thee to graciously bestow upon me Thy heavenly blessing. Purify my thoughts and actions so that they may be guided and directed by Thy divine wisdom. Believing that all things are possible in Thy Name, I beseech Thee in all humility to fill my whole being with love, compassion and understanding for all those who come my way. Bless me with true knowledge and the ability to receive Thy everlasting love into my soul, so that I may sincerely seek out the truth in Thy Holy Name. Help me to rise above my own earthly concerns and to inspire those who are in need of Thy love and guidance at this time. Thank you, Father, AMEN.

Break the Pack

Tarot cards are like mirrors of the soul, reflecting knowledge and wisdom. To keep their vision crystal clear, you must handle them correctly, so that they are not clouded by indistinct or irrelevant spiritual impressions. This is the reason for "breaking the pack."

Whenever you have used your cards for study or divination, it is necessary to disperse any previous energies by thoroughly shuffling the pack before you wrap it in the Tarot Cloth and put it away in its wooden box. Then, when you are ready for a new reading, remove the pack, carefully unwrap it and hold it between your palms in an attitude of prayer while you recite the previous INVOCATION. Now you are ready to "break the pack" and work with the client. As you perform the break and shuffle the cards, you are also demonstrating to the client how it is to be done by him.

The more you work with your cards, the more responsive to outside energies they become, and I recommend strongly that you break the cards both before and after each reading. Let me give you an example from my own experience.

I was once given a purse I had admired, and I used it to carry my Tarot cards, pad and pencil. After doing this two or three times, I realized that I was receiving an impression of insecurity, which would leave as soon as I had broken the pack. I became curious and asked the friend who had given me the bag about this. She explained that once someone had attempted to take the bag from her in a department store, and it was only because she had the strap securely on her shoulder that the would-be purse-snatcher did not succeed. But this experience upset her greatly for a while and she had feelings of insecurity every time she went out with the purse. But eventually these emotions subsided and she had forgotten the incident entirely when she gave me the bag. Even long after, her feelings of insecurity had been transmitted to my cards through the purse. "Thoughts are things," and the amazing sensitivity of the Tarot had picked them up!

Have the Client Perform the Preliminary Procedures

In order to ensure the proper rapport and flow of esoteric energies between you and your client, explain to him clearly and directly the procedures he is to perform before the actual divination can begin. After you have chatted with the client for a few minutes to put him at ease and you are correctly seated at the table; after you have removed your deck from the cloth, repeated the Prayer of Invocation and broken the pack; and after the client has written down his question or "Wisdom of the Tarot" and placed it before him:

1. As you break the pack, tell the client that you are going to ask him to shuffle and cut the cards.
2. After you have shuffled the cards for a few moments, hand them to the client and tell him to shuffle them just as you did, or in any way he desires. Tell the client to concentrate intensely on the written question or "Wisdom" request as he shuffles.
3. After the client has shuffled the cards for a few minutes, tell him to cut the deck into three stacks, still concentrating on his question. Holding the deck in his left hand, he releases a certain number of cards; then moving from right to left, he releases a second stack; to the left of that, he releases the remaining cards in a third stack.
4. Then instruct the client to pick up the three stacks with his left hand, starting with the first stack at his far right, then the center stack, then the last stack.
5. Now tell the client that you will be reading the cards in the position that they are handed to you, so at this point he may either turn them around or hand them to you just as they are.
6. Take the cards from the client, being careful to keep them in the same position he gives them to you, and perform the final procedure before actually commencing the spread, the Ritual of Solidification.

Perform the Ritual of Solidification

Like many others in this Handbook, the Ritual of Solidification is a very old procedure, handed down through many ages. "Solidification" means to make or become solid, to crystallize, to become strong or united.

When you receive the pack from the client, hold it firmly between the palms of your hands and press gently three times, in the name of the Father, the Son and the Holy Spirit. This act of faith unites with strength the wisdom to be received from the Divine Trinity of God.

You need not do this little ritual openly; it is performed in silence and dignity, yet it is a very inspirational gesture and the perfect way to strengthen the channel to the Higher Self.

Commence the Spread

Once the Solidification is completed, you are ready to commence the spread. It will take some time and practice before you can decide quickly which spread is most suitable for the type of question asked. In the next chapter, you will find a limited number of spreads described. I have found that too wide a choice presents difficulty for the apprentice; you will find the number of spreads given quite sufficient for any situation.

A good Tarot reader should be in no hurry with a divination. Earlier in this study I explained that there is far more to the Tarot than individual cards. Take plenty of time to understand how the cards interact with each other — look for the overall message. As you place each card in spread position, try to sense the totality of the vibration; try to tune in to the "links" which will guide you in understanding the connections among all the cards. Before you begin to interpret the spread, try to sense the general feeling of the spread as a whole. This will help you considerably when you begin the individual interpretations. Let your fingertips gently caress each symbol; as your sensitivity develops you will feel the thrilling sensation of the varying esoteric currents. Learning the Tarot is like learning another language; communicating on a higher level is invigorating for both mind and body. It is a beautiful language, and once learned can never be forgotten.

CHAPTER 11
HOW TO READ THE CARDS

Every day of our lives, our minds receive thousands of bits of information and impressions, all of which are stored away in mental cubbyholes, some for future use, some to be "forgotten" forever. But they are all there, with more being added all the time. This becomes quite a mental clutter, unless we can develop the concentration to retrieve only what we need when we need it.

This is particularly true of the Tarotologist, for you must not only be able to recall bits of data — facts and information — for each reading, but you must summon up the wisdom to make decisions and interpretations based on the material before you. Your mind can easily become confused and disorganized, especially if your client's thoughts are not properly directed as well, and this confusion and disorganization can seriously affect the veracity of your reading. This is the reason for having the client write out his question and concentrate on it, as outlined in the previous chapter.

But what about you? There is a device which I have found to be extremely useful in focusing your own concentration, as well as that of your client, during a divination. With the help of this simple aid, you can direct your spiritual attention to the higher energies you wish to contact and release yourself from the muddle of normal thought patterns.

Using the Lemniscate

The *Lemiscate* is a very ancient and powerful symbol: in mathematics it is the symbol for Infinity and resembles a figure eight lying on its side: ∞ In occult teaching it symbolizes both Eternity and Infinity and is often used to depict Cosmic Consciousness. It can be clearly observed, for instance, over the heads of the figures in THE MAGICIAN and STRENGTH in the Rider Waite Deck.

By drawing a Lemniscate in black ink on a piece of white poster board, as shown on page 220, you can provide yourself with a simple but effective means of focusing concentration and eliminating much of the distortion of negative or confusing vibrations.

LEMNISCATE FOR DIVINATION

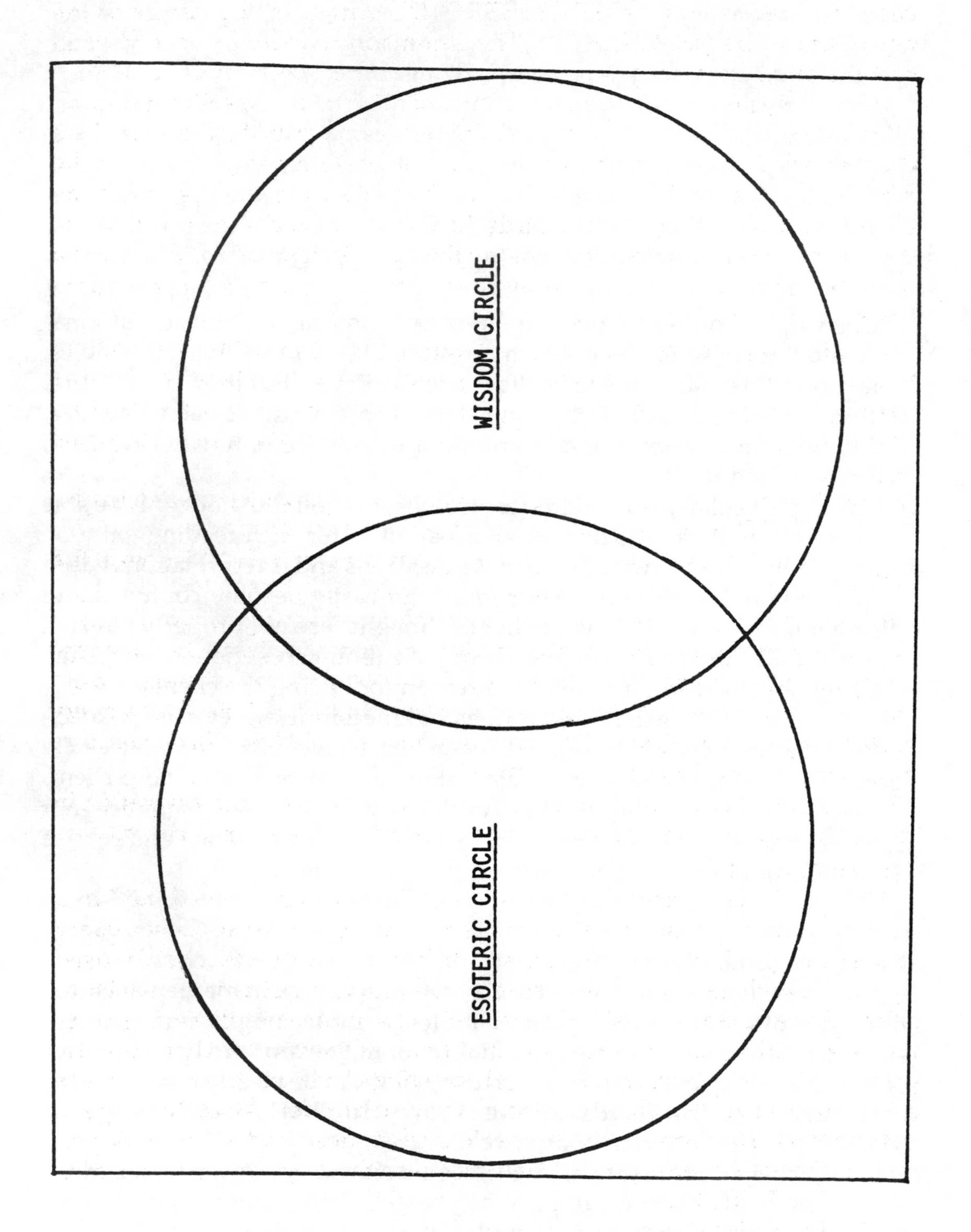

CHART 7

The Lemniscate should be drawn as two interlocking circles, side by side, with the words "ESOTERIC CIRCLE" written in the center of the left-hand circle and the words "WISDOM CIRCLE" written in the center of the right-hand circle (see CHART 7). The Lemniscate should be used with all spreads and kept with your Tarot deck and other tools for divination.

After the client has written his question, or if no specific question, "Wisdom of the Tarot" on a piece of paper, as described in the previous chapter, and is concentrating on the question or statement, he is given the cards to shuffle. Still concentrating on the paper, the client shuffles the cards thoroughly, then cuts the cards three times, restacks them and hands them back to you. As you perform the Ritual of Solidification, you ask the client to continue concentrating on the paper until he feels that his query has been absorbed into the Tarot deck.

Usually the client will be anxious to get on with the reading and will not take much extra time at this point. Now instruct the client to fold the question paper twice, so that when it is opened the fold makes a cross which forms four squares. The client then places the folded paper into one of the two circles of the Lemniscate.

1. If the client has a direct question, the paper is placed in the ESOTERIC CIRCLE.
2. If the client has no specific question and has written "Wisdom of the Tarot," the paper is placed in the WISDOM CIRCLE.

(This same procedure is followed when you are reading for yourself.)

After the divination is completed, and the client feels satisfied that the query has been satisfactorily answered, you should remove the paper from the circle, tear it twice along the two folds and dispose of it. Each new query requires a new paper, and the previous paper should be destroyed before beginning a new spread.

Also remember to shuffle the cards thoroughly after each divination in order to clear them of the vibratory "imprint" of the former client.

The Tarot Spreads

A "spread" is a particular formation of Tarot cards "spread out" in a definite order and sequence to obtain esoteric insight into the client's query or desire for guidance. There are many different spreads which can be used by the Tarotologist, and the nature of the enquiry determines which to select. Some spreads are simple and others are quite complicated, getting into areas of Karmic responsibility and other advanced concepts. For the purposes of this Handbook, I will describe three spreads which are adequate to cover the types of readings you will undertake at this stage in your studies. They are the types most frequently used and will provide you with sufficient versatility in divination. These three types of spreads are:

1. The Celtic Cross
2. The Celtic Block
3. The Predictive Manteia

The Celtic Cross

This is the most commonly used spread and is a very ancient method of reading the cards. It will provide hours of intriguing study, and you will be amazed at how ten cards can relate so much information. The Celtic Cross can be used to answer questions that require some background or general knowledge.

Throughout this Handbook, I have repeatedly emphasized the need for becoming sensitized to the meanings of the cards themselves; now it becomes important as well for you to thoroughly learn the different spreads, so that you can lay the cards out in the correct order, concentrating on the cards themselves, rather than where you are placing them.

Ten cards are used in the Celtic Cross Spread. The first card is placed over the folded piece of paper with the client's query, which is in one of the two circles of the Lemniscate. As you lay out each card, you should say aloud firmly what each one represents:

1. This is what covers you.
2. This is what crosses you for good or bad.
3. This is the basis of the situation.
4. This is behind you, or in the process of leaving.
5. This is what crowns you and could come into being.
6. This is before you.
7. This represents your own negative feelings.
8. This represents the feelings of others around you.
9. This represents your own positive feelings.
10. This is the outcome.

Lay out all ten cards and complete the spread before attempting to interpret the cards. Don't hurry — take your time and observe everything you can before relating any information to the client. Take into consideration the Suit Keys, a profusion of any one suit, the balance of the spread and the number of Court Cards. When you are still new to divination, it is perfectly all right to make notes to aid you in determining the message. Keep in mind at all times the client's question or whether the Wisdom of the Tarot has been requested. Get the feel of the spread and allow your intuitive powers to arouse your sensitivity before revealing anything to the client.

On the next page, you will find a diagram for laying out the ten cards of the Celtic Cross. Remember, when laying out *any* spread, keep the cards close together and the formation neat. This helps considerably in making the vibratory flow of the spread smooth and potent.

On page 224 you will find an exercise which will explain the meanings of each of the ten cards as laid out in the Celtic Cross Spread. Study this exercise until you are thoroughly familiar with each card's meaning, as you may often be called upon to explain them to a curious client.

CELTIC CROSS SPREAD

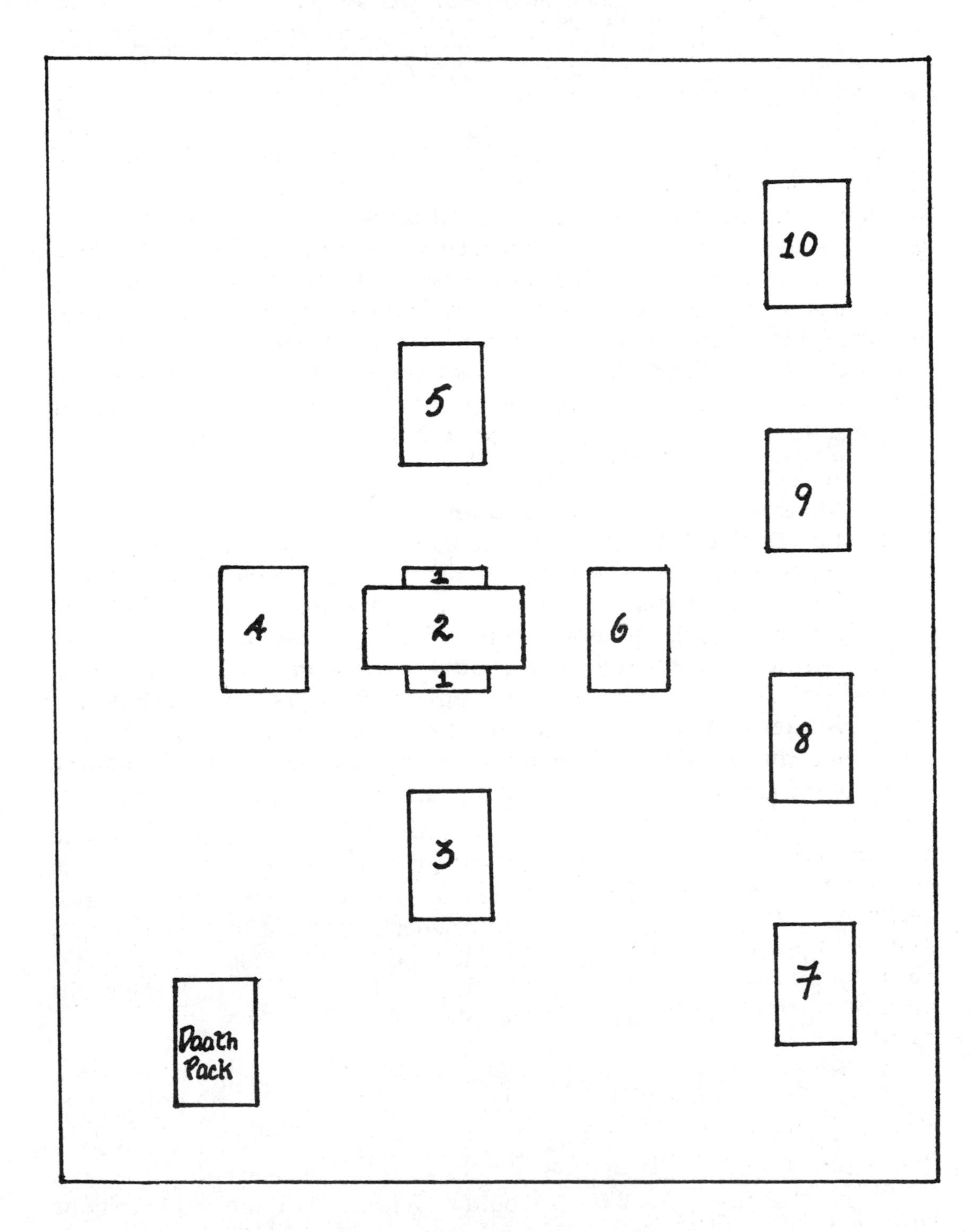

CHART 8

EXERCISE 11: ANALYSIS OF THE CELTIC CROSS

1. **This is what covers you.**
This first card allows you to go beyond the client's question. It tells you what he is experiencing in regard to the question. The vibrations surrounding the condition are revealed in this first card. If a Court Card turns up here, it indicates that another person is involved in the client's query.

2. **This is what crosses you for good or bad.**
Whatever this card represents can be determined in the light of the remaining spread. Whether it is favorable or unfavorable depends upon the card itself and the client's question. For example, if the question has to do with the success of a new business enterprise, and the Ace of Wands turns up in this second placement, we can assume that it crosses the first card favorably. However, it is always better to scrutinize the entire spread carefully before offering an interpretation.

3. **This is the basis of the situation.**
This card reveals the real origin of the client's question. The written query usually does not indicate the whole situation, so you should pay special attention to this card. If, for example, a female client asks whether a certain man will contact her, you may find that the third card reveals a quarrel in the client's past or a long journey of separation. There could be many reasons for her question, and this card will tend to reveal them to you if you are perceptive and intuitive. The third card will help you considerably in your overall divination.

4. **This is behind you, or in the process of leaving.**
From this card you can see the immediate background of psychic vibrations experienced by the client. Depending on the client's attitude, the condition indicated may still be with him. If this condition is an undesirable one, a word of encouragement to the client may help to dispel the situation, for the fourth card indicates that it is in the process of leaving or clearing up. If the card is favorable, the remaining cards will indicate this.

5. **This is what crowns you and could come into being.**
The fifth card relates to situations not yet materialized and so is extremely helpful in advising the client. With this card you can see a possible — and often probable — course of future events. If you can tell that these possibilities would be harmful or undesirable to your client, you can advise him accordingly. Likewise, if the possibilities seem beneficial, you can gently encourage the growth of the seed contained in this card.

6. **This is before you.**
In the process of interpreting this card, you should consider the tenth and final card also. These two cards have a positive relationship and are connected in the final interpretation: one leads to the other, and both deal with a future situation that is taking shape as a result of past and present circumstances.

7. **This represents your own negative feelings.**
I have known students to be very confused about this card. What happens if a positive, promising card turns up in this position? It simply means that the client has a negative attitude toward this situation and cannot appreciate or accept the beneficial circumstances indicated. You can be of great assistance to your client when reading this card; you can offer guidance and often relieve him of his anxieties regarding the situation, so that he can come to accept whatever benefits are in store. Also, together with the third card, this seventh card can help you to see deeply into the true emotions surrounding the client's original question.

8. **This represents the feelings of others around you.**
If the client has asked a question involving another person, this card will help you to see the other person's point of view. However, if the question relates only to the client's activities, the eighth card provides insight into how other people feel regarding the client and his situation.

9. **This represents your own positive feelings.**
Often a person thinks one thing, but through fear or inhibition says another. The ninth card will help you determine how the client *really* feels about the matter in question. If he is apprehensive, you can guide him toward the solution to his dilemma through the wisdom of the Tarot.

10. **This is the outcome.**
The tenth and final card indicates the outcome of the situation. Its interpretation depends upon the people and circumstances involved in the client's question and upon the nine preceding cards. All the other cards lead up to this card and must be read accordingly. You must first arrive at a conclusion, based on the totality of these factors and your own intuition, then you must decide what action to recommend to your client, based on your thorough understanding of the spread in relation to the client's question.

Second Readings

After you have analyzed the total message revealed by the spread, there are several situations that may arise which necessitate a second reading:

1. **When the last card is a Court Card:**
   When a Court Card appears in the tenth position, it is indicative that the answer to the client's question relies upon or is associated with a person whose characteristics are typified by this card. In this event, you should first help the client to identify the person indicated; then retrieve the Court Card, place it on the table in position number one and hand the pack back to the client for reshuffling. Commence a new reading, placing card number one over the Court Card. When the client is asked to reshuffle the cards, also ask him to concentrate on the person represented by the Court Card, rather than on the original question. By following this procedure, you are able to continue the reading, and the first card dealt will indicate what covers the relationship or situation between the client and the person represented by the Court Card.
2. **When more information is required:**
   Sometimes a spread can bring to light a situation or aspect about which the client would like more information. In this case, you should follow the same procedure as described for the Court Card, i.e., extract the card that prompted the enquiry, place it in the first position, and after the client has reshuffled the cards while concentrating on the *new question,* place the first card over the extracted card, saying: "This is what covers *this* situation."
3. **When higher guidance is indicated:**
   After the ten cards have been laid out in the Celtic Cross Spread and *before* you commence the reading, notice the total number of Major Arcana cards in the spread. If there are *four or more* cards of the Major Arcana, the spread should be picked up immediately and the 22 Major cards extracted from the pack. The spread should then be continued, using the Major Arcana only. (If you have a separate pack used only for Major Aracana readings, this may be used, but remember to have the client shuffle them first.) Four or more Major Arcana cards in a spread indicate that the client needs help from the higher level of the Wisdom of the Tarot, whether he knows it or not. If four or more Major cards turn up *before the spread is completed,* do not continue, but follow the procedure just discussed. By using the Major Arcana only, the message related will be more profound and of much more benefit to the client. He should be advised that the nature of the cards indicates that there is a more significant message awaiting him in the Major Arcana.

The Daath Pack

When a spread has been completed and before you commence your interpretation, you should place the cards remaining in the deck to *your left side* (see Chart 8). This pack is then known as the DAATH PACK, which means "wisdom not yet received."

As your studies progress, you will use many different spreads that call for continued use of the cards from the Daath Pack, so it is advisable to practice the correct procedures regarding these cards from the beginning. During the reading, the Daath Pack should not be handled by anyone except you and your client, when you find it necessary to have him reshuffle the cards for a second reading, as discussed above.

The Celtic Block

This spread is actually a continuation of the Celtic Cross. The preliminary procedures are identical to those used for the Celtic Cross, and the first ten cards are laid out in the same manner.

At this point, you place the Daath Pack to your left and commence your interpretation of the spread. After your reading has been given and is understood by the client, you then pick up the Daath Pack and, working from *right to left,* place cards 11, 12 and 13 below and beneath cards 6, 3 and 4 (see Chart 9). These three cards form what we call the TRIAD.

Triadic Divination

This extension of the Celtic Cross coordinates with the previous ten cards and confirms the knowledge you have already gained from them. To complete the Celtic Block, card 14 is then placed to the right of card 11 and beneath card 7. This card is known as the SOLIDIFIER: it brings out, or solidifies, all that the spread conveys. Together, the Triad and Solidifier represent a deeper area of information conveyed. It is up to you to combine the wisdom gained from the Cross with the Triadic vibration in your interpretation, which should contain a vibratory force identical to that condensed into the final card, the Solidifier. The Solidifier should verify all your previous conclusions.

You must remember that the Celtic Block is a separate spread from the Celtic Cross. You cannot commence a Celtic Cross spread, then decide to add the Triad and Solidifier. You must decide before spreading the cards which layout to use; this will depend upon the client's need and question. Usually the Celtic Cross will provide all the information required, but if you should wish to delve further to extract more detail, you may proceed by taking the card the client wants more information from and beginning a new spread, as discussed above, this time using the Celtic Block. By doing this, you can confirm your conclusions through the added dimension of Triadic Divination.

CELTIC BLOCK SPREAD

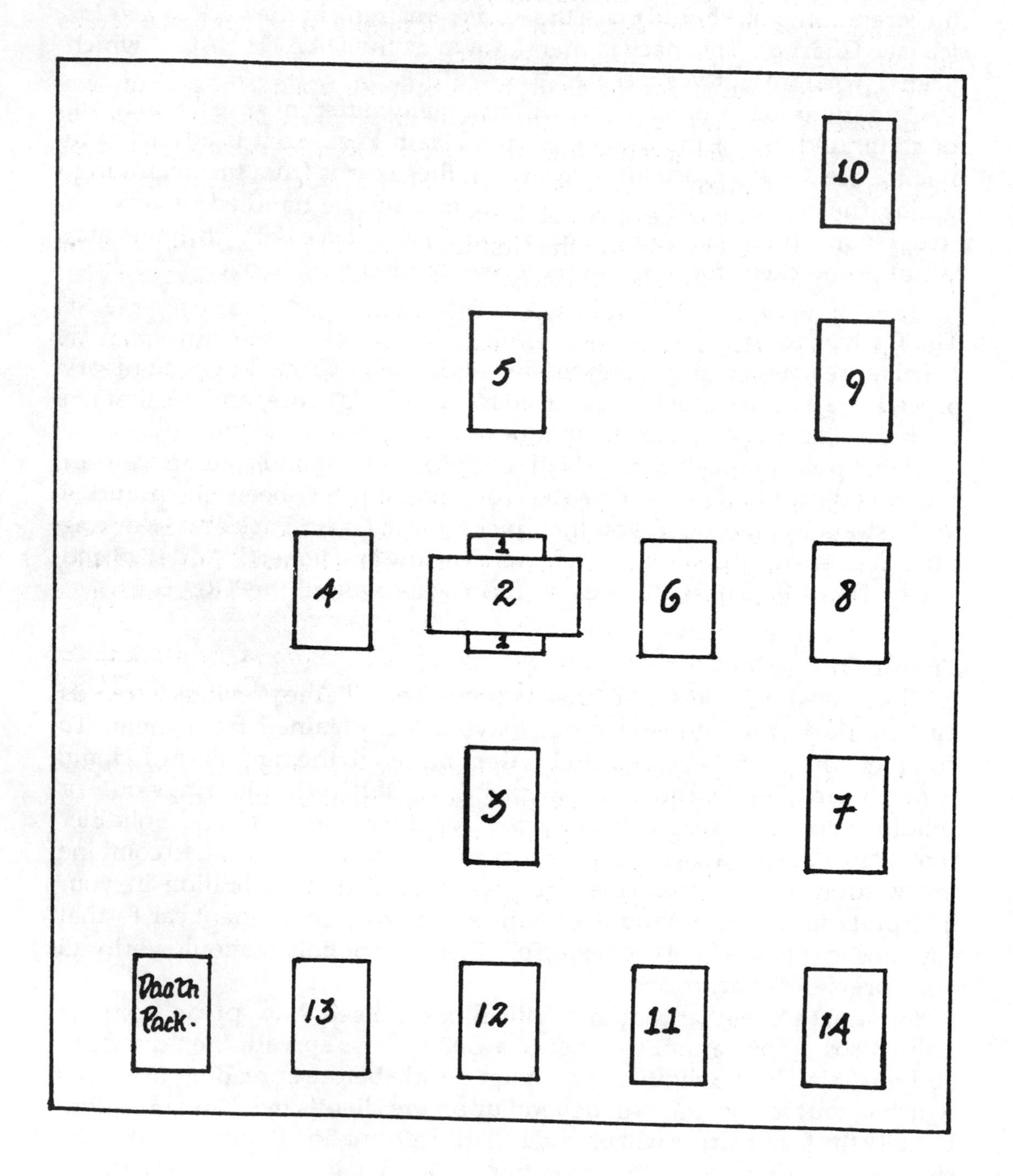

CHART 9

The Predictive Manteia

This spread enables the Tarotologist to go into greater depth of divination and gives in fuller detail the root vibrations and vibratory forces surrounding the client during the reading.

As with the Celtic Cross and Celtic Block Spreads, follow the preliminary procedures. You may find it helpful with this more complex spread to prepare a placement chart like the one on page 230, with rectangular areas large enough to accommodate the cards. Such a chart is easily prepared with black ink on a large sheet of white poster paper.

Begin the spread by placing the first three cards in the positions of the PAST, PRESENT and FUTURE TRIADIC SOLIDIFIERS, as shown in Chart 10 as positions 1, 2 and 3 respectively. This divine triad in the center of the spread provides the nucleus from which emanate cosmic energies that are channeled into particular categories to provide esoteric keys for interpretation of the cards.

The cards are placed in these positions in the following manner:

1. After the client has shuffled the cards and cut them into three piles, instead of having the client recombine the piles into one pack, *you* take the first card from the top of the stack to *the client's right* (your left) and place it in the position of PAST TRIADIC SOLIDIFIER.
2. Then take the second card from the top of the *center* stack and place it in the position of PRESENT TRIADIC SOLIDIFIER.
3. Finally, take the third and last card from the top of the stack to *the client's left* (your right) and place it in the position of FUTURE TRIADIC SOLIDIFIER.

In the process of placing these three Triadic Solidifiers, you should recognize the Divine Trinity whom they represent by saying:

Card 1: In the name of the Father . . .
Card 2: And of the Son . . .
Card 3: And of the Holy Spirit. Amen.

PREDICTIVE MANTEIA SPREAD

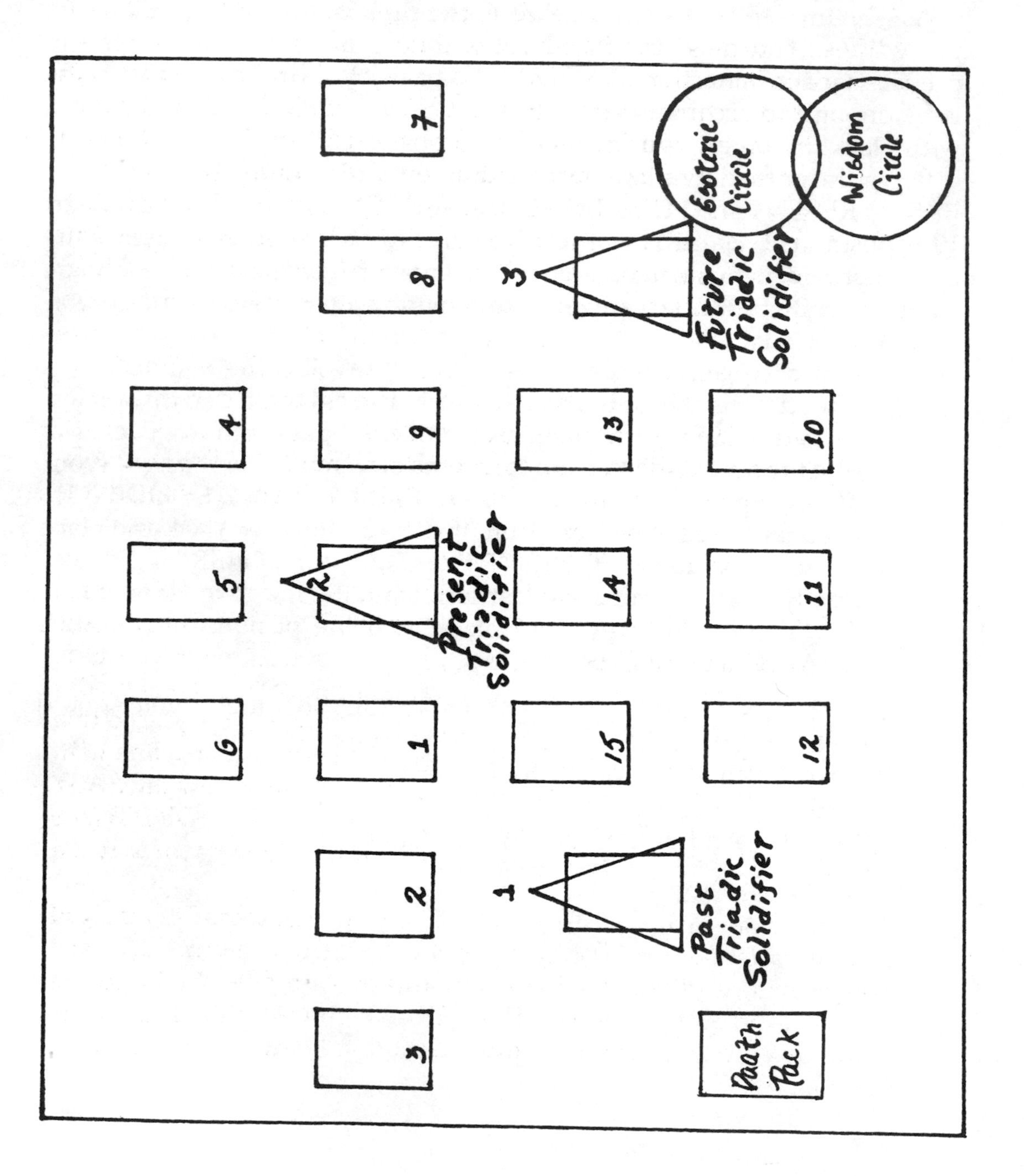

CHART 10

Blocking the Triads

After the initial three cards are placed, you may begin filling in the remainder of the spread, or "blocking the Triads." Proceed as follows:

1. Starting with the stack of cards to the right of the client (your left), bring the three stacks together into one pack.
2. Proceed to block the FIRST TRIAD by placing the next three cards in a row from right to left, to the *left* of the PRESENT TRIADIC SOLIDIFIER, as shown in Chart 10. These cards are 1, 2, and 3 and represent the vibrations surrounding the client during the reading.
3. Interpret the full Triad before proceeding to the SECOND TRIAD. The first three cards will give you a solid background on the client and provide a strong basis on which to proceed with the reading. Interpret each Triad separately in turn, to the satisfaction of the client, before going on to the next. During interpretation, place the DAATH PACK to your left, on the edge of the spread (see Chart 10).
4. Cards 4, 5 and 6 are next placed in a line from right to left directly *above* the PRESENT TRIADIC SOLIDIFIER, as shown in Chart 10. Card 5 should be centered above the PRESENT TRIADIC SOLIDIFIER. Now interpret this Triad, which will enable you to recognize the true, root vibrations of the client's query or need for guidance.
5. The next Triad is made up of cards 7, 8 and 9, placed in a line from right to left, to the *right* of the PRESENT TRIADIC SOLIDIFIER (see Chart 10). From this group of cards, you can determine the esoteric direction the client must take in order to achieve necessary goals.
6. The next Triad comprises cards 10, 11 and 12, which are placed in a line from right to left toward the bottom of the spread, in a line with cards 4, 5 and 6 at the top and between but slightly below the PAST TRIADIC SOLIDIFIER and the FUTURE TRIADIC SOLIDIFIER (see Chart 10). These cards will indicate the level of achievement that can be expected.
7. The last Triad, made up of cards 13, 14 and 15, allows further insight into the previous Triad of expected level of achievement. Each card will provide additional information and explain how the indicated level will be brought about. The vibratory forces of the final three cards link up with those of the preceding Triad in the following fashion:

   Card 10 = Card 13
   Card 11 = Card 14
   Card 12 = Card 15

Cards 13, 14 and 15 are placed in a line from right to left between and slightly above the PAST TRIADIC SOLIDIFIER and the FUTURE TRIADIC SOLIDIFIER, lined up directly above cards 10, 11 and 12 (see Chart 10). This completes the spread.

8. After the full spread of 18 cards is completed, the three Triadic Solidifiers should confirm your reading with the following relationships:

PAST TRIADIC SOLIDIFIER (1) = Cards 4, 5 & 6 should correlate with this Solidifier to show past vibratory forces dealing with the client's question.

PRESENT TRIADIC SOLIDIFIER (2) = Cards 1, 2 & 3 should correlate with this Solidifier to confirm the client's present situation.

FUTURE TRIADIC SOLIDIFIER (3) = Cards 10, 11 & 12 should correlate with this Solidifier to show the client's future activities.

9. Cards 13, 14 and 15 are *not* associated with the Triadic Solidifiers because this part of the divination does not necessarily deal with the future — it may deal with events in the past or present as well. It informs us of the experiences the client may undergo prior to the "achievement" level.
10. Cards 7, 8 and 9 present us with the Wisdom of the Tarot and advise the immediate action the client must take in order to bring about the results seen on the achievement level. The direction received from these cards is the best of all, for the client's past activities have been taken into consideration here.

The apprentice should study the Predictive Manteia step by step, carefully and intently, before attempting a serious spread. This layout takes a little longer than the other two spreads but it gives added depth to the reading. Unlike the two Celtic spreads, the Predictive Manteia cannot be continued, for it is complete in itself. The three spreads given in this Handbook contain sufficient depth for your use at this stage of your experience. The more you use them, the better you will become at interpreting them correctly and easily.

During your early work with these spreads, keep a record or log of your study spreads, including the questions asked. This will enable you to determine quickly which spread is best for the type of query received. (See Chart 1 in Chapter 1 for a good format for recording your spreads.)

Once you understand why a particular card appears in a certain position, you will be able to concentrate far better on the divination itself. Be sure that whatever query you present to the Tarot is clear and written down. Don't rush yourself — give your intuitive powers time to respond and guide you in your interpretations.

CHAPTER 12
THE ESOTERIC TIME CARDS

The subject of time in relation to the Tarot is one which has always been considered difficult by Tarotologists. When we consider that the ancient masters had no hesitation whatever in using the symbols to determine time, we must ask ourselves why the modern Tarot reader tends to avoid including time in his divinations.

I believe that the answer lies in the hectic pace of life in our contemporary world. In the more peaceful atmosphere of bygone days, people lived their lives at a much slower pace. Today we are under all kinds of pressure from so many directions that doctors are kept busy prescribing pills to calm us down and help us cope with the speed of modern living.

In this fast-moving age, we are affected both physically and psychically by everything around us. Take away the cars, aircraft, radios, television sets and telephones and what would happen? We would slow down again! We would become more in touch with ourselves, have more time for introspection, relaxation and serious thought. Most of us have lost sight of our inner being in today's world — we are so busy keeping up with everything that we never consider the truly fundamental questions of our lives.

Try this experiment: ask yourself the following three questions, repeat them several times, think about them seriously:

1. Who am I?
2. What do I want in life?
3. What is my purpose here?

What has all this to do with time? The answer is everything. When you endeavor to assess the time factor in your spreads, you will find that your ability to do so is affected by the condition of your mental and spiritual vibrations. In order to determine time accurately, you must have inner balance and harmony in your own life. You must know who you are, what you desire, and why you are here, at least to a greater degree than the ordinary person. When you have become more spiritually balanced, through your studies, prayers and meditation, you will become more sensitive to and aware of time as we know it here on earth.

The accuracy of forecasting time also depends largely on the inner balance of the client; however, by achieving your own sense of spiritual balance, you can overcome a client's negativity to a certain degree and assess the time factors involved with a greater degree of accuracy.

A strong *positive* attitude of the client produces an effect on the cards that can result in your predicting a *premature* time factor.

A strong *negative* attitude of the client produces an effect on the cards that can result in your predicting a *delayed* time factor.

Time is an important element in divination and one with which your clients will often be concerned. They will wish to know not only *what* is likely to occur, but *when* it is likely to occur. This chapter, therefore, will give you some of the rudiments of working with the cards in predicting time factors. It is a lengthy study in all its ramifications and longer than we have room to cover here. As you progress in your studies, you will be able to learn more about it, but here you will find all you need to know at this stage of your advancement. The basic time procedures we will study will apply to the Celtic spreads only.

NOTE: Unless the client specifically requests a time factor in his written question, *do not* concern yourself with it *unless* you are already sufficiently advanced in your studies to be able to relate to the time cards with ease and without detriment to the overall reading.

The Season Cards

The four ACES are the Season Cards:

ACE OF CUPS	= SPRING	= March/April/May
ACE OF WANDS	= SUMMER	= June/July/August
ACE OF SWORDS	= AUTUMN	= September/October/November
ACE OF PENTACLES	= WINTER	= December/January/February

Although the Aces are Season Cards when they appear in certain positions in a spread, they also retain their individual interpretations as well. Don't become so involved in trying to determine a date that you lose the essence of divination contained in each card in the spread!

Aces play an important part in the Tarot drama. When an Ace appears in a spread it opens up many possibilities in terms of interpretation. EXERCISE 3 in Chapter 2 provides a good deal of important information about the Aces, and if necessary, it might be a good idea at this point to go back and review this material before going ahead.

Relating the Season Cards to the Celtic Spreads

The important positions in both Celtic spreads concerning time are cards 5, 6, 7, 8 and 9. Here is what they represent:

Card 5 = This is what crowns you and could come into being.
Card 6 = This is before you.
Card 7 = This represents your own negative feelings.
Card 8 = This represents the feelings of others around you.
Card 9 = This represents your own positive feelings.

When the client's query involves a time factor and there is an Ace in any of the above five positions, it indicates the time of the year involved. For example, an Ace of Swords falling in position 6 means that the event will occur in the autumn — sometime between September and November.

Determining the Week

Having determined the *season* of the event concerned, we now look to *Card 10* — the outcome — for the key to the *week* of the event. Let us say that the Three of Cups appears in position 10, with the Ace of Swords in position 6. This means that the event will culminate approximately *three weeks* from the beginning of the autumn season, or about the third week of September.

Although the Aces are important in all five of the Celtic positions, the two most revealing esoteric time cards are

Card 6 = This is before you.
Card 10 = This is the outcome.

Card 10 — the Date Card — is a fixed aspect. The *number* of the card that falls in this position determines the *week* of the event, within the confines of the Season Card in positions 5, 6, 7, 8 or 9.

Now let's study in detail each of the positions in which the Aces, or Season Cards, may fall.

TIME CHART

POSITIONS 5-6-7-8-9 = SEASON CARDS (ACES)

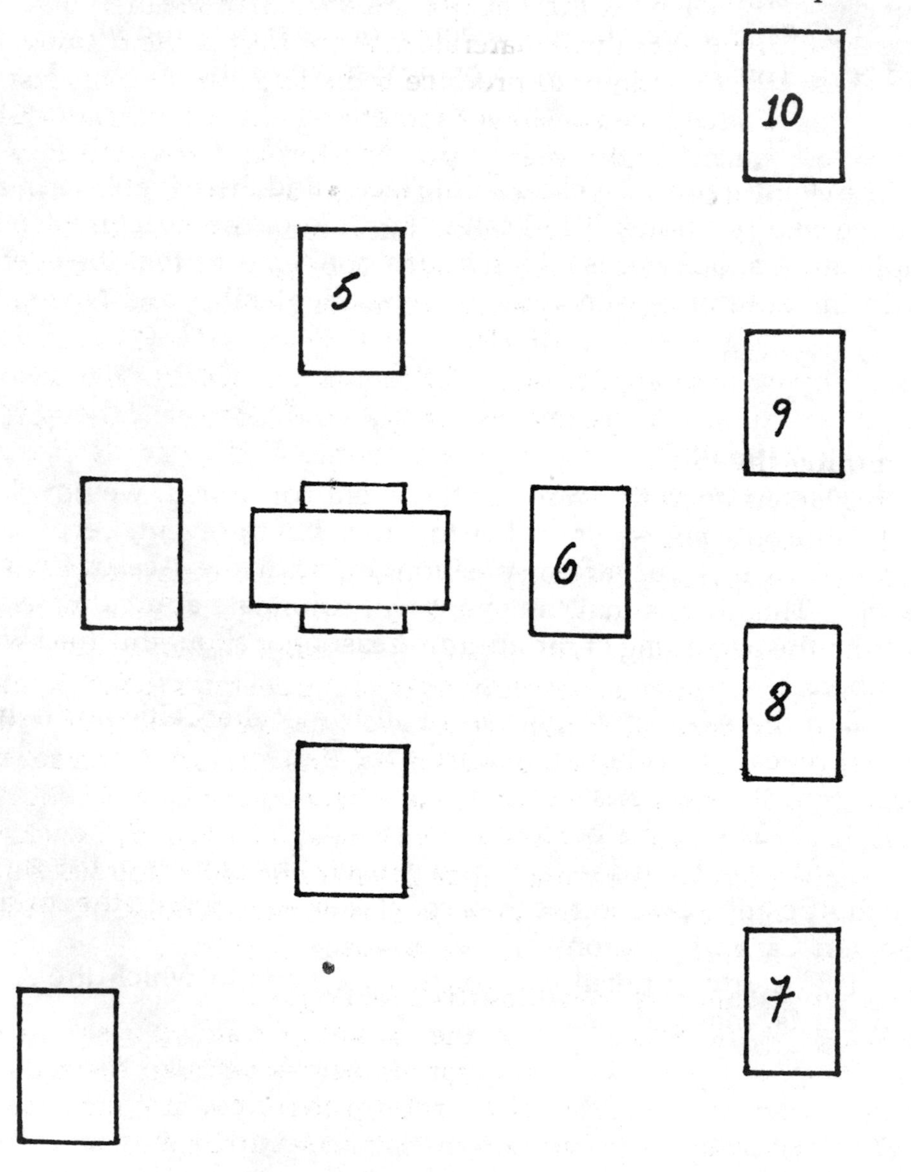

CHART 11

5. **This is what crowns you and could come into being.**
When the Season Card appears in the fifth position, it must be read as part of the whole spread first. After you have interpreted the entire spread, you may then attempt to determine the time element if the client has requested this specifically. A Season Card in the fifth position indicates that if the situation under consideration continues to evolve in the same manner and with the same vibratory energy that surrounds the client at the time of the consultation, then you may assume that the event will materialize according to the reading. But the client must continue to produce the energy and enthusiasm to effect this result. Once a desire for something has been implanted into the ether, that thought energy projects forward into the possible future and will continue to grow and mature as long as it is assisted by constant mental effort. Like a plant that is cared for constantly, it will bloom into reality; but if the thought energy is not maintained, or becomes weakened and polluted by negative fears and doubts, the desire may not materialize at all. Indeed, this force works both ways: your fears may materialize instead! Positive thought energies produce positive results; so as "corny" as it may sound, keep your thoughts on as high a positive vibration as possible and your desires *will* materialize, sooner or later.

6. **This is before you.**
The Season Card in the sixth position makes the possibility of the event occurring at the time you predict far greater. This is because it indicates that the client has already determined the time element to a great degree by previously applying positive energies to the situation. Remember that not all future events likely to occur because of positive energies directed toward them are *themselves positive!* A future event may actually be negative in itself, but positive thinking will contribute to its materialization also, just as with a positive event. By developing your sensitivity and spiritual capability in divination, you will be able to guide your client through these sometimes difficult distinctions and keep him on the path he really wants to follow.

7. **This represents your own negative feelings.**
In analyzing the Season Card in the seventh position, you should take time to contemplate the entire spread before defining the time element. When the Season Card turns up here, you are immediately confronted with a negative thought barrier set up by the client. It may not necessarily represent a negative attitude toward the time factor connected with the query, but nevertheless, negative vibrations fight against the natural rhythm of events proceeding to their conclusions. So it is up to you to try and determine the balance of the entire spread and the amount of influence exerted upon it by the Season Card.

8. **This represents the feelings of others around you.**
The Season Card in the eighth position is encircled by an entirely different type of vibration: that of other people who may be involved in the situation under consideration. However, these vibrations are channeled through the client and are influenced by his reactions to them. Reading the time factor in the eighth position is fairly straightforward, but you must be aware that the event will come to pass as the Season Card forecasts, in association with or through the activities of another person or persons. The client is only a part of this future event.

9. **This represents your own positive feelings.**
In the ninth position, the Season Card must be considered carefully as an integral part of the entire spread. How it relates to the whole is very important in this position. You must determine the nature of the positive energies surrounding the event, as projected by the client, and ascertain whether or not they are in harmony with the client's query regarding the time factor. Your advice and counsel to the client in these circumstances can be of immense value, physically and spiritually, and can help him to channel his future life path constructively.

From the foregoing material, you can see that the Season Cards are activated in any of the five positions from 5 through 9 in the Celtic Spreads. The time element is modified somewhat according to the position in which the Season Cards appear.

You should practice placing the Aces, or Season Cards, in the various Celtic positions and learn to master the subtle vibration that defines time. It is an important ability to possess in serious divination and your clients will often ask you to predict time factors in your readings. Before you attempt to forecast time elements for clients, however, you should practice with self-divination. Through time, concentration and serious study you can learn to master this ability with remarkable accuracy. It is exciting and encouraging to be able to forecase events with a reasonable degree of success and can be of great help to your clients.

Determining the Day

Determining the exact *day* upon which an event is likely to occur requires the use of a basic procedure from Gnothology, or esoteric Numerology. This is more involved than merely predicting the season or week; you must first obtain the client's PERSONAL LIFE CYCLE.

Numerology teaches that each number has its own vibratory frequency and level of spiritual power. Each human being has his own vibratory cycle, based on the numerical values of the numbers associated with the year and month of his birth.

In Numerology, all compound numbers are reduced to a single digit, except for master numbers 11, 22 and 33. For example, the number 49 = 13, which reduces to one number, 4.

To arrive at the Personal Life Cycle of an individual, we first determine the CHRIST CYCLE for the current year in this simple fashion:

$$1980 = 1 + 9 + 8 + 0 = 18 \qquad 1 + 8 = 9$$

Thus, the CHRIST CYCLE for 1980 is 9. Each year everyone is under the influence of a different Personal Life Cycle. The number of this cycle, once you have the Christ Cycle number, is determined as follows:

Christ Cycle for 1980 = 9
Month of Birth = 7
Day of Birth = 16
32 = 5 = Personal Life Cycle

Once we have the number of the client's Personal Life Cycle, the next step is to determine the INDIVIDUAL DAY CYCLE, in order to calculate the time element desired. This is done by adding the number of the Personal Life Cycle to the MONTH AND DAY REQUIRED by the Season Card and Date Card in the Celtic Spread. Here is the entire procedure, in step-by-step form:

Let us say that the client has a question regarding time. Ask him for his date of birth. Say that it is May 4. Add the *Christ Cycle* for the current year (1980) —9— to the month of May, whose number is 5, plus the date of birth, which is 4. This adds up to 18, which reduces to 9, the number of the client's *Personal Life Cycle.*

1. The Season Card is the ACE OF SWORDS, which represents the autumn months of September, October and November. It can appear in any of the Celtic positions of 5, 6, 7, 8 or 9.
2. The tenth card is the fixed aspect, the Date Card. It is the THREE OF CUPS. From the Date Card you can assess the MONTH and the WEEK: Three weeks from the beginning of the autumn season is the third week in September.
3. Now you can calculate the client's INDIVIDUAL DAY CYCLE by adding his PERSONAL LIFE CYCLE number (9) to the number of the month involved, September (9). This gives us a total of 18. Now the missing factor is the number of the particular *day* in the *third week of September* which when added to 9 will give us the INDIVIDUAL DAY CYCLE number of 3.
4. You simply add the numbers of the dates of each in that week until you come to the one that totals a number reduceable to 3. This would be September 21 (2 + 1 = 3):

   Personal Life Cycle = 9
   September = 9
   Date = 21
   39 = 12 = 3 = INDIVIDUAL DAY CYCLE OF 3

To summarize: The Three of Cups in the tenth Celtic position is the Date Card, a fixed aspect. From the Date Card you can assess the week and day of an event. The numerical value of the tenth card is *three* in this case, indicating the *third* week of the month revealed by the Season Card, the Ace of Swords. By ascertaining the client's Personal Life Cycle number, you can then calculate the client's Individual Day Cycle, which will be a day in the third week of September whose numbers equal three. When this date is added to the client's Personal Life Cycle and the number of the month, the total will reduce to three. This verifies for the client the date upon which the event in question is likely to occur.

If No Season Card Appears

If your client has requested a time element and no Aces appear in the spread, the Wisdom of the Tarot indicates that the client needs more knowledge regarding the situation queried. It may be that some adjustment in attitude or circumstance is necessary before the actual time can be revealed, or perhaps vibratory forces are working toward a goal not yet known to the client. Often when the original query is reworded or rewritten, you can spread the cards again and this time find the time factor. If a Season Card still does not appear in a second spread, the query should not be pursued further at this time.

If a Court Card Appears in Tenth Position

When a Court Card turns up in the tenth Celtic position and a Season Card is in the spread, this denotes that a person with the Court Card characteristics is involved in the event in question. You would then proceed to find the next numbered card by going back through the laid-out cards in a systematic manner, i.e., 9, 8, 7, etc. The first numbered card you come to will then serve as the Date Card.

If a Major Arcanum Appears in Tenth Position

When a Major Arcana card turns up in the tenth Celtic position, a deeper significance is added to the query. You should inform the client of the more profound energies involved in this situation. A Major Date Card indicates that higher cosmic forces will be active on the date in question and that this day will be more meaningful than usual for the client. The numbers of the Major Arcana cards should be reduced to one digit for purposes of calculation: The Sun (19), for example, would not indicate an Individual Day Cycle of 19, but rather of 1 ($1 + 9 = 10$; $1 + 0 = 1$). Likewise, the *first* week of the season would be indicated, not the nineteenth.

If the Date Card is Reversed

If a regular numerical card appears in the tenth Celtic position, but is reversed, this does *not* necessarily indicate any negativity connected with the day in question. The Reverse Key of the card will, however, have some bearing on the date, and the spread should be interpreted accordingly (see Minor Mentors for Reverse Keys).

Tarot Ethics

You have now almost reached the end of your apprentice journey into the beautiful and profound world of Tarot. You have come to possess a degree of accuracy in divination that includes not only general and specific interpretations of events, but the actual times they are likely to occur. This is knowledge of a high order—and with knowledge comes power. How this power is used is the beginning of wisdom, for with knowledge and power comes responsibility. And the responsibility of the Tarotologist is always to God, to his Higher Self and to the welfare of his client.

Remember that the Tarot always reveals what the client *needs* to know—not necessarily what he *wants* to know. This can often be confusing for the apprentice reader. If your client has posed a vague question or has asked one thing but really feels the need to know something else, the spread will reveal this. It is advisable, therefore, to inform your client of this fact; it can help to eliminate thought barriers and confusion.

Suit Key Significance

If four or five cards of the same suit turn up in the first ten cards of a Celtic Spread, you should become aware of the influence of the *Suit Key* in interpreting the spread. However, it is not necessary to explain this element to the client. The Tarot is so penetrating and reveals so much depth when properly utilized, it is not always wise to explain every facet of this wisdom to the client. If you try to do so, especially in an attempt to impress him (or her), you may burden the client with more than he needs to know and keep him from concentrating on the question at hand.

Using Discretion

When you receive guidance from the high planes of consciousness, you should be constantly aware of the awesome privilege you are enjoying and never attempt to take advantage of the situation. To do so could be disastrous for both you and your client. If you foresee circumstances of a highly personal nature, you should avoid this area unless encouraged to explore it by the client. A sensitive and responsible reader will offer subtle guidance but never attempt to expose or embarrass a client in any way. Always endeavor to help the client in the most positive manner, without undue stress to the client's emotional sensitivity.

When you are able to sense impending events that may have serious negative effects on a client's life, your first thought should be to help him find ways to avoid these situations. Don't dwell on negative probabilities and remember that no matter how closely they can be pinpointed, they are still only probabilities, not certainties, until they occur. Remember that prediction, no matter how expertly done, is never 100 per cent accurate, for free will always enters into everything we do, constantly altering the future. Divination is only the art of forecasting events that are *likely to occur if nothing is done to change them*.

But often a client is not able or willing to exert the effort required to change a probability, and it does indeed occur. For this reason it is especially important that a Tarotologist *never* predict death, serious accident or any other catastrophic situation. This would be unethical and disastrous.

Absent Readings

Unless you have received a direct request from a client, you should never attempt to spread the cards for him without his knowledge or permission. It is doubtful that you could obtain a meaningful reading, and this type of conduct is unprofessional and irresponsible. If you *are* asked to read for someone in his absence, I recommend that you obtain a photograph of the subject and before commencing the spread spend a little time "tuning in" to the vibratory forces surrounding the picture. The reading is then begun by placing the first card *over the photograph* and saying, "This is what covers you."

CHAPTER 13
BEGINNING AND END

You have now reached the conclusion of this basic study of the Tarot. Within this Handbook I have offered you many keys to the wonder and mysteries of this Sacred Science, the fruit of my many years of teaching, studying and meditating. I hope you will use them wisely and well to add beauty and meaning to your own life and the lives of others.

There is much to learn about this intriguing science, and as you progress and deepen your studies with constant cultivation and exploration, I hope that the Tarot will come to mean as much to you as it has to me. It has been my hope that this Handbook will provide you with a solid foundation and the basic tools needed to launch you into a serious study of the cards and their beautiful and powerful symbology, and that through this study you will find ways of pursuing your personal goals of spiritual enlightenment. The more you reach up toward your Higher Self, the more questions you will have about your true nature and the place you occupy in God's infinite universal plan.

The Way of the Tarot is full of sunshine and lights up many other spiritual pathways for the seeking soul as well. In the golden light of inner wisdom you will discover, as others have before you, that the Royal Road of Tarot leads always Home.

INDEX OF CARDS

This Index is intended to enable you to refer quickly to the Mentors for each card in the Tarot deck. The page numbers refer **only** to the Mentors and not to other references to specific cards throughout the Handbook.

MINOR ARCANA

Wands	Cups	Swords	Pentacles
Ace, 77-78	Ace, 89-90	Ace, 109-110	Ace, 125-126
Two, 79	Two, 91-92	Two, 111-112	Two, 127-128
Three, 80	Three, 93-94	Three, 113-114	Three, 129-130
Four, 81	Four, 95-96	Four, 115-116	Four, 131-132
Five, 82	Five, 97-98	Five, 117-118	Five, 133-134
Six, 83	Six, 99-100	Six, 119-120	Six, 135-136
Seven, 84	Seven, 101-102	Seven, 121	Seven, 137-138
Eight, 85	Eight, 103-104	Eight, 122	Eight, 139-140
Nine, 86	Nine, 105-106	Nine, 123	Nine, 141-142
Ten, 87-88	Ten, 107-108	Ten, 124	Ten, 143

COURT CARDS

Wands	Cups	Swords	Pentacles
King, 146	King, 151	King, 155	King, 159
Queen, 147	Queen, 152	Queen, 156	Queen, 160
Knight, 148	Knight, 153	Knight, 157	Knight, 161
Page, 149	Page, 154	Page, 158	Page, 162

MAJOR ARCANA

0 The Fool, 164-165
1 The Magician, 166-167
2 The High Priestess, 168-169
3 The Empress, 170-171
4 The Emperor, 172-173
5 The Hierophant, 174-175
6 The Lovers, 176-177
7 The Chariot, 178-179
8 Strength, 180-181
9 The Hermit, 182-183
10 Wheel of Fortune, 184-185
11 Justice, 186-187
12 The Hanged Man, 188-189
13 Death, 190-191
14 Temperance, 192-193
15 The Devil, 194-195
16 The Tower, 196-197
17 The Star, 198-199
18 The Moon, 200-201
19 The Sun, 202-203
20 Judgement, 204-205
21 The World, 206-207